Dedication

To my Minister, the Honorable Minister Louis Farrakhan. We love you and hope you will accept our work. Our souls delight in serving you! You have done your job so well and so exquisitely that we deserve the chastisement if we fall in this hour.

Preface

This is a book about blended families and it provides a wealth of information to the reader. Blended families are formed when adults in a new relationship decide to live together. Children of one or both partners may live with the couple full-time or come to visit. Blended families can work well and provide lots of love, security and support for children and parents. We all know the false narratives that America pushes about the black community. One of those it that we don't want marriage and we want to shack up and be reckless. We have met so many couples that not only want marriage but want to know more about it. We are going throughout the country trying to build understanding and help couples to see how they can make it. Please take this as a serious read to help you with your blended family. We don't believe in "step" anything. You will not find that language in this book. We want to help you to successfully blend your family. The Honorable Minister Louis Farrakhan in his article, Rebuilding the Family said, **"In order for us to make a new family, we have to return to Him who created the man, the woman and the family and we must be willing to accept His Thoughts and His Ways."** Hopefully this book is helping us to do just that. You will not successfully blend your family without God at the helm.

- Brother Marcus and Sister Cecelia

Tip # 1

There are three questions that you must answer together after you get into the process of your marriage. The first question is **what will our family culture be about**? Before getting married, you may have prioritized family time over other activities. As a single man or woman, you may have spent weekends with just your children. You may have made pancakes in your pajama's, blew bubbles on your deck, and stayed up late reading together. You may have ventured out often, to art museums and local parks. Your weekends belonged to you and your family, stretched wide open to be filled as you liked in the moment.

Your spouse's family may have been totally different. Maybe they were deeply rooted in the community. Maybe they were very active in the church or mosque, and the four of them spent most of Sunday on the go to services. Their Saturdays were dedicated to sports and school activities. It was important to your spouse that their children were involved in activities, and they often juggled an impressive pick up and drop off calendar.

That difference, hardly noticeable when we were courting, came screeching to the forefront of our married life. Maybe you feel rejected when your assumptions did not happen to be your marriage reality. Did you enter a Blended Family relationship and not talk about everything before you got married? So many of us do!

In relationships, assumptions can be very destructive. I once heard a story about the negative effects of assumptions. This woman told a story of how she had prepared a list for her husband of several items she needed at the store. She thought it made sense to number the list – and assumed that her husband would benefit from the numbers: item number one, item number two, etc. Unfortunately, her husband thought that the numbers on the list meant the number of items. He bought one bag of sugar, two bags of flour, up to twenty bags of 20-lb dog food. Now, they can laugh at this story, but think about what probably happened once he got home. She was furious at his lack of sense, and he was furious at her assumptions and not taking the time to be clear about what she meant.

When another person assumes incorrectly what we mean, or assumes something about us, we don't often think **"Well, that's a reasonable assumption."** Instead, we think, **"What is wrong with them?!"** While we all make assumptions throughout the day (and some research shows we are wrong better than 50% of the time) we can, at times, be annoyed with other people who do it to us.

Sometimes we make assumptions because we simply don't have the time to think something through or do an analysis and check for understanding. We might be on the highway and our partner says, **"Turn here"** and we think they mean the next exit, when maybe there was a side road running off the highway and that's what they were referring to. It would not be practical, at 60 miles an hour, to turn and ask them, **"What do you mean, exactly?"**

However, in our normal day-to-day lives we often don't stop and take the time that we should to inquire about what someone else means or is trying to say. We don't practice active and reflective listening. Active listening is when we seek to understand, more than wanting to be understood. We ask questions, we probe for what's underneath a person's statements, and we engage until we have our own personal **"Ah-hah!"** about what the other individual is trying to communicate. This is what we should have done before we got married to our spouses but maybe we didn't.

The family cultures your respective families came from may have varied in a hundred other ways. You may had read to your children nightly before snuggling them into bed. Your spouse may have simply kissed their children goodnight and shut the door. Maybe they served dessert at night, but you never did. Maybe they encouraged their children to play outside on sunny days, but you don't mind yours being all sprawled out on the floor building with Legos or listening to music.

As you discover the differences in your family cultures, the temptation is to sometimes get stuck on the lens you viewed it through rather than just observing and talking about it. Each of these choices is appropriate; it's the value and implied message we assign to them that made each of us uncomfortable. Sometimes we can be uncomfortable talking about the things that are important to us in our own marriage. You must know that statement is true for your spouse as well. Are you unnecessarily making it hard for them to talk about anything in the marriage or relationship? Encourage your spouse to always share what's on their heart. The more they speak, and you listen you get a look into their minds. Maybe you didn't discuss your family cultures more explicitly before you got married. Maybe it would have avoided hurt feelings and more than a few arguments. Now you can work on talking more about the reality of the marriage and dialogue about what you would like to see.

Tip # 2

What do we expect of a Blended Family Mother or Father?

You never really know what you are going into with a blended family situation if you don't ask. Does your spouse keep the children every day or do they have an arrangement with an ex-spouse or girlfriend? You must ask so that you will know. On days when you and your spouse have the children, you will have to meet them on behalf of your spouse to cut down on the confusion. The object is the making of peace and the doing of good. You will be stretched many times as a Blended family Mother and Father. If you expect the children to like you immediately you might have to go back to the drawing board several times. They most likely will not give you the proper respect or love until much later if you hang in there.

Tip # 3

How will we manage our money?

Sometimes, because we don't communicate well, we leave may issues on the table. Sometimes, because we don't know how to resolve issues and be done with them, we have seemingly endless discussions about things AFTER we get married. One of these discussions is how are we going to handle the money? Is what you make considered our money? Is what you make considered your money? Sometimes we gloss over things. We breezily agreed to share money equally before we said I do. We each worked and supported our families prior to our marriage and saw no reason to keep our money separate. Now we are in the process of marriage and this issue keeps coming up. The simple exercise of budgeting nearly derails many blended families. We must be honest about money. So many of us have never had real money and it has the potential to drive us crazy. Set a realistic budget and financial goals. Don't justify purchasing something you can't afford.

Maybe you both have spending categories that your spouse won't support. **Managing money with our co-parenting partners further complicated the issue**. Again, be honest about what's going on in your life. Sometimes you must talk several times to reach a solution.

What are the spending priorities in our relationship? What kind of pre-existing commitments exist that must be considered? What kind of arrangements have already been made? What can be changed in favour of our new, blended family marriage? Do everything with the thought of it favouring your new relationship with your new spouse. Be mindful of any creeping resentment that you have once you have agreed to things.

Everyone should have some financial freedom. Whether $5 or $500, discretionary income is a must for any partnership. If you want to run it through a shredder, it ought to be your right to do so. Having your own money helps you feel like you haven't given yourself up in order to be part of a relationship.

While financial independence is important, it must be balanced with accountability. Don't hide your spending habits from your spouse. Live within the boundaries you set. You should consult your spouse before purchasing big-ticket items.

Don't live a fairytale! Get real about how much money you have. Emotional problems can't be solved with money. Take a hard look at what's really behind your spending habits.

Don't let yourself get taken advantage of. Are you working 80 hours a week just so your spouse can live beyond your means? That's not being a partner; that's being a paycheck, and it won't fix the problem. Negotiate, and then renegotiate when necessary. You made these life decisions together, and you can change them together.

Educate yourself. Marriage is a partnership, and both individuals need to be well-informed. Many problems — especially when it comes to money — stem from lack of knowledge.

When a financial issue comes up, ask yourself: Is it really a money problem or is it a relationship problem?

Money should not be used as a weapon against your partner.

We recommend both joint and separate accounts. We recommend a joint account to put money in for the bills and separate accounts for your own discretionary money.

Tip # 4

Dreaming is a healthy and wonderful part of the romantic days before a couple forms a family. In first families, the dreaming can continue beyond the honeymoon. For blended families, because their lives are already very much in progress, reality hits as soon as the families share a household. Don't expect your families to meld together overnight. It can take one to four years for blended families to adjust to the changes. But parents who are proactive in reducing and addressing potential problems can make the adjustment period smoother. Through the adjustment new roles in the family must be set and this will likely result in conflict and arguments. For example, one child is used to be the oldest in the household and now he has a half-sibling that is a couple years older it will take them awhile to figure out the **"peaking order"** for the house again. The family is not only adjusting to the remarriage but also to the whole process of a pervious divorce or separation, one-parent family set-up, the parent courting a new partner, and finally the adjustment to the remarriage. The issues left unresolved for the children or the parents will likely show back up as the parents move towards remarriage. For example, a child who seemed fine with the new partner is now acting out with their blended family parent due to having to put to rest the hope their biological parents would get back together. This is one of the main hopes of the child or the children. The main thing with a blended family is communication. You can't sweep stuff under the rug and hope it will be ok. Covering questions before you get married will help to save you from endless arguments and helped you to avoid resentment.

Tip # 5

The latest U.S. Census data reveal that our children will be growing up in a different world than we did. What does that mean for our children and their future? You must teach your children to respect everyone and the various languages that people speak. Don't think that what you say and do doesn't affect your children. The respect that you show for other cultures will probably be exactly what the respect your children will show. Teach them the importance of speaking and knowing Spanish. They will need to know Spanish in the world that is coming in. They also need to know and be aware of the many different language that are spoken in the world. English is fine, but will they know just English? How will they play and dialogue with the children of Africa if they know just English? In some countries no one speaks English. So, teach them so they will know. Get your education up on the way others in the world do it and speak it so you will not be lost.

Tip # 6

Teach your children to respect Grandmother and Grandfather on both sides of the family. Not just yours, but your spouses too. Bring them over to both sides of the family as much as possible. Each them what life is and what death is. This starts with you having respect for them. Do you have unresolved issues with mother or father? A lot of our trouble in successfully blending families starts because there is not a lot of respect for anything that proceeded us. Respect everyone and everything in your Blended Family marriage. Especially the ones that preceded you into your spouse's life. All their family was in their life before you came along. Show respect. Respect means that you display a warm, positive feeling or action towards someone or something considered important. You hold them in high esteem or regard. You convey a sense of admiration for good or valuable qualities and by honoring them you exhibit care, concern, or consideration for their needs or their feelings. This is what you must do for all the members of your spouses' family from this point on. If you want to be successful.

Tip # 7

National surveys of remarried couples with children rate children as the number-one cause of conflict between them. Sometimes you have a blended family and you play favourites. Your spouse can see the way you interact with your children and the way you interact with their children. Your spouse be watching you avoid their children. Maybe your spouse is available to help you're your children's homework and maybe they watch TV with them, and maybe they are steadfastly present with your children even though your children prefer interacting with you exclusively. Maybe they are more committed to the welfare of your children than you are to their children. Would you prefer that your spouse leave your children alone and have little contact with them? Maybe your spouse can see what you can't see, or you refuse to see. This requires honesty on your part.

Tip # 8

Give Your Spouse Authority

Often, children have difficulty accepting the authority of a stepparent, especially in a newly blended family. As your spouse's partner, you can encourage your child's cooperation by giving your spouse authority — in the presence of your child — to enforce specific rules. After the child witnesses his parent granting this authority, the stepparent can remind the child of the biological parent's rules and can seek compliance from the child.

Tip # 9

Have Closed-Door Negotiations

When you disagree with your spouse, keep your conversations and negotiations behind closed doors, especially when it involves child-related issues. Stepchildren are naturally skeptical about a new stepparent and will resist rules or changes a non-biological parent has initiated, even though they may have accepted these changes from their own parent. Present a united front for the children. Unity is easier to achieve when the Blended Family parent allows the biological parent to take the lead.

Tip # 10

What are some of the top rules that you have for your blended family household. Remember that the children of whatever you set up but you should meet privately as a husband and a wife to have a general sense of things. They must all be rules that everyone can adhere to, and the children must know them. Here are some to consider:

Rule: Everyone must Be Kind and practice Kindness with one another

We must practice being kind to each other and outside our walls. Kindness means the quality of being friendly, generous, and considerate. When was the last time we were kind to someone? Ask the children how are they kind? We must use kind words with each other. Don't allow words like hate to come up and you not challenge it and talk about it when your children or others use it. Talk about kindness in the news, kindness at school and work hard to demonstrate kindness at home. Ask your children, can they recall a time when somebody was kind to them? Change the scenario and think of a time when they were kind to another person? You would be surprised at how foreign this concept is in this generation. Challenge your own concept of kindness. You must move into your heart and notice the feelings there. In this fast-paced world, kindness and compassion takes a back seat to selfies, self-interest and expendable human interactions. Every person is waiting to be discovered or become rich, believing it holds the key to their happiness. Yet when they attain success, they long for their former life having underestimated the trappings of fame and celebrity. The plain fact is that the planet does not need more successful people. But it does desperately need more peacemakers, healers, restorers, storytellers and lovers of every kind. It needs people who live well in their places. It needs people of moral courage willing to join the fight to make the world habitable and humane. And these qualities have little to do with success as we have defined it. Kindness is fundamental to the human existence. We are thrust into the world as newborns and enriched with the kindness of our parents' nurturing for the ensuing years. Humans are the only mammals with a prolonged gestation period. Other creatures rely on support for a brief time before becoming self-reliant. We are powerless at birth and depend on our caregivers to provide for our needs. Therefore, kindness is sewn into the framework of our DNA. We are literally wired for kindness. Every person has opinions on how to improve the world, though no one wants to practice kindness in their own backyard.

Tip # 11

Rule: We're One Team

We eat together whenever possible. We travel together. We talk about our blended family history and make up funny combined blended family names. We share chores and space on the sofa. Going into the marriage with a willingness to work and communicate will help the relationship. Instant adjustment is not realistic for everyone, so remind yourself to be patient. The goal is unity and a sense of belonging to a group, not exclusion.

Tip # 12

Rule: Respect Privacy

A closed door requires a knock. Children aren't allowed in each other's rooms unless explicitly invited. If you are asked to leave a room, you must, and quickly. Toys in a room are for the exclusive use of that child, and we never require sharing. They must want to share but not be forced to share. We don't post pictures on social media without explicit permission from the subjects. We don't discipline children publicly, and don't talk about anything remotely negative about a child (a tough test score, a failed audition) in front of the others. This creates trust and helps the children learn about boundaries.

Tip # 13

Rule: Work, then Play

The children are responsible for a fair amount of their own care and keeping. They clean their own rooms, they help with meals, and they manage their own laundry. You must teach your children in your blended family. In the mornings, we expect them to get dressed and eat breakfast on their own. Many pack lunches or get sports paraphernalia ready for practice in the afternoon. They complete their homework independently. All that happens before the TV turns on or the crafts come out. This rule is a real game changer.

Tip # 14

Rule: You Do You, But Don't Cramp Others' Style

There's room to breathe here. Children can be anyone they want to be. Encourage your children to go out and face life! The same God that you depend to keep them safe in the house will be out there for them as well. This extends to their day-to-day life. Don't like what we're having for dinner? Don't eat then or go by yourself the meal you would rather have. If your dinner is ready on time to eat with others and you clean up your mess, it doesn't really matter. Had a rough day? So sorry to hear that. Hang out on the couch listening to your moody music to your heart's content. But if you snap at your sister? Take your storm cloud to your private room, please.

Tip # 15

What Happens When a Rule is Broken?

When a rule is broken, gently correct and move forward. Like in all families, sometimes a rule is broken egregiously or repeatedly, and requires a consequence bigger than removing the child from the situation. In those instances, **the parent leads and the stepparent supports.**

If the drama includes more than one perpetrator, as it often does, listen to each side of the story in front of the offending parties. We then discuss privately and return with your decision.

Know that you must navigate new situations and establish consistent boundaries.

<u>Tip # 16</u>

Everyone Needs Attention

What's the Issue? When the number of children increases, as it frequently does in blended families, one or all the children might feel like they're not getting the attention that they're used to. Additionally, blended families sometimes have less time and money for each child's extracurricular activities or for family outings because of the increase in family size. As with so many other issues, this problem can be resolved—to the best of its ability, anyway—by working together as a family. Create a set schedule that everyone has weighed in on, with each child choosing an activity within a certain budget throughout the month.
Additionally, both adults should attend each child's activities, such as sporting games, plays or concerts, so it doesn't feel like any child is being favored over another.
Give each child individual attention as well. Whether you play a quick game together for 10 minutes every day or you schedule a once-a-month outing, giving biological children and Blended Family children plenty of **positive attention** can strengthen your bond.
Tip # 17

Blended Family Discipline Can Be a Challenge

Sometimes the only solution we have is to whip a child's behind. Sometimes it warrants that and sometimes it doesn't. Sometimes the discipline can cause quite a few problems in the household. Whether it's your child or someone else's child discipline rules should be set. No one should be beating on your child nor should you be beating on someone else's child. Ask the biological child's parent how they would like to see discipline of their son or daughter handled. They may tell you that they don't want you touching their child. You must decide whether you can live with that or not. Some of us can't take not being able to discipline a child especially if we are the ones responsible for their upkeep. Perhaps the biological parent should handle their own child and that option should always be on the table. If it is your own children, then a family meeting is in order. Before this meeting takes place, sit down with your partner to **determine your household rules**. Sometimes we can be married and not want our spouse to say or do nothing that looks like discipline to our child. Maybe you have spoiled your children so much out of guilt that you couldn't bear any discipline to take place. Be honest with your new spouse. Do you really expect them to give your children a pass when they break the rules? Take notes and write down your rules and the consequences for breaking those rules. If you both have children already, there's a good chance you have somewhat different rules. So it's important to come together to create the same rules for everyone so that you don't **live like two separate families under one roof**. Identify **how you're going to discipline** and what type of consequences you're going to use. It's imperative that the two of you **present a united front on disciplinary issues**. Sometimes, one parent wants to be the **"fun one."** At other times, one parent hopes the new parent can lay down the law and get things on track fast. But coming together as a blended family means both parents need to work together as a team. Remember, children quickly learn who the **"easy target"** is when it comes to getting their way and can grow to be masters of manipulation to pit one adult against another. Call everyone to the table. Take out those notes that you jotted down and go over them as a family.

Your young ones might have some thoughts that they want to contribute and having it all written down means that everyone will know exactly what the household rules are, as well as the consequences for breaking those rules.

Explain to the children that, in your house, both adults can enforce consequences to any of the children, and it's expected that the children will obey the other parent as they would any other authority figure.

With all of that said, it's important for parents to focus more on building a bond rather than disciplining the children initially. Without a healthy relationship, discipline won't work. This is especially true with adolescents.

Tip # 18

You Feel Like Two Separate Families

You and your new spouse want to feel like one unit that can have fun, share, and rely on each other. The children aren't entirely comfortable with each other, though, nor with their new parent. It feels like you're still acting as two families that just happen to live in the same house. Remember you can't forge a bond overnight. It will take to time to gain a shared history, figure out new relationships and adapt to the new normal. Start the process slowly by beginning new traditions as a family. They might be reading a book together every night in the big bed in the master bedroom or taking a trip to the local playground every Sunday morning before breakfast.

You can also smooth the transition of going from house to house, a process that might happen regularly if you or your spouse have joint custody. For example, you could stop for ice cream every time you pick up the children from the other parent's house. This little tradition signals to the children that it's time to move into a different routine, but in a fun manner.

It's also important to give children time to grieve. While a new marriage can be happy, it also signals the end of the previous family dynamics. And that can be tough for children who are still struggling to deal with the fact that their **biological parents are no longer together** or that their time of being an only child with heaps of attention has come to an end.

Despite problems, a blended family is still just that—a family. Although there might be growing pains, squabbles and a few moments of discipline, everyone will eventually adjust to the new situation. Mistakes will be made, by children and by adults, but everyone will learn from those mistakes. Eventually, the household will feel less like a mish-mash of families and more like one solid unit.

Tip # 19

Bookkeeping

Practically speaking, only one person should keep the books. Even though one person primarily handles balancing the checkbook, both should be fully trained and able to do it.

There is nothing wrong with the wife handling the finances in the family if she is the better administrator, but God still holds the husband accountable for the ultimate decisions.

When there is an impasse, the wife must yield to her husband and allow the Lord to work it out. As they work together, encouraging one another, God will show them His favor and grace.

Nevertheless, being responsible as the leader does not mean the husband is a dictator; the couple should discuss and agree on financial management.

Both spouses should be involved in paying the monthly bills. Doing so will keep both fully aware of their financial status. Neither should go off secretly and do things that will bring serious financial harm to the family.

Within a marriage relationship the husband and wife are partners who are dedicated to one another.

A bond of uncompromising devotion creates a healthy atmosphere for togetherness: studying God's Word, praying, and even managing money.

Just as it takes two to make a marriage successful, it takes two to establish a clear line of communication in financial planning.

Tip # 20

' Raising a blended family comes with its share of obstacles. In the United States, approximately one-third of all households are blended. With patience and a positive attitude, the blended family can be one filled with love, respect, and admiration.

It isn't easy for the children when parents remarry. They are caught in the middle of a situation that can cause immediate feelings of frustration and discontent. At its root, every family has a different dynamic. The trick to making a blended family work is finding a new, combined dynamic that includes time spent together, discipline, and rules BOTH parties can live with.

Here are a few tips to make your blended family one of peace and harmony:

Be patient! Just because the adults are in love, that doesn't mean the children will immediately feel the same emotion. Many children, no matter their age, believe the universe revolves around them. If this sounds like your children, they will not be able to understand your choices. They can also feel jealous and insecure, especially at first, as they cannot predict how things will be. It won't happen overnight but getting to know one another and learning to live together, happily, takes plenty of trial and error. Try to maintain an adult, emotional mindset. Children can be hurtful toward a new parent. Stay above comments like **"You are not my mom/dad."** Avoid being emotionally manipulated. Remember, as an adult in a blended family, it is up to you to be mature.

BLENDED FAMILIES

woven together by choice
strengthened together by love
tested by everything
and each uniquely ours

Tip # 21

Make the children feel safe! Children want their opinions to count and want to feel stability. In blended families, children are often filled with uncertainty, mistrust, and fear. Reassure them often and don't make many demanding changes at once.

The children are not in a honeymoon period of love! Make sure they still have plenty of time to be seen and valued in their relationship with their parent. If the children feel pushed aside, they will likely take it out on the new parent, causing friction and chaos.

Don't force the children to respond too quickly. A child should not be forced to call a new parent mom or dad or connect with him/her.

Allow the children to hug, share nicely, and build relationships in their own time.

Tip # 22

Set limits and boundaries. Things are new, uncertain, and emotionally taxing. This doesn't mean the children should start calling the shots. Parents need to be clear of their expectations for behavior, discipline, and rules, applying them to all the children to keep things in order. The children may not respect or appreciate a new authority in their life right away, but in time – with persistence and patience – they can learn to be respectful. Being respectful means listening to the opinions of others without comment if you know they are set in their ways and won't change anyway. It's standing up for your own beliefs even though they may run counter to the opinion of the herd. You must learn to respect your children and they must grow to respect your opinions.

Tip # 23

Speaking of respect, you must make sure each child is respected for who they are and what they feel! Never make children choose between, or talk badly about, their **"real"** mom or dad. It can be difficult to make a blended family work if the children feel they must choose sides. Remember that your children are really under no obligation to be super close to the person you choose to marry nor their children. While that's hard to accept, they must respectful – they don't have to love them. Encourage respect, communication, and empathy. Working on the respect for the whole family is important. That means watching the tone of conversations and being hyper-sensitive to what things are like for the other people in the relationship, especially the children. Although you can't force the children and Blended family parents to love each other, you can set an expectation for considerate behavior and communication. Respectful communication even more important in a blended family because you have so many new dynamics that are playing a part.

Tip # 24

A blended family can be a wonderful thing. When successful, the children can be empowered to know and love people they may have never met. Keep in mind: In a blended family, surface issues may seem like one thing; however, they could likely be something else. Give it time, compassion, and consideration. You might find that your blended family is better than you could have ever imagined.

Tip # 25

A blended family is not picking up where the other marriage left off. It is a brand-new creation with new players and new parameters and therefore needs new rules. Instead of trying to fit the new people, places, and situations into the old mold, design something new. Blending a family requires time. Bringing two families together is a long-term investment. Keep in mind that the divorce rate increases for people who get married a second time around. Look at blending a family as a long-term goal rather than a quick fix. You must prepare yourselves for the long haul. In the early stages of the relationship, couples feel excited and spend a lot of time together. You're re-falling in love again. Especially for those coming out of a loveless marriage, this feels wonderful. You go from divorced in-love. You have hope for the future. You're spending so much time together because it feels good. Strive to make what you feel now last throughout the relationship.

Tip # 26

Handling questions from your children

"Mom, are most divorced people like you and Dad, or do they usually hate each other? I think most divorced people hate each other."

Children see adults who once loved each other fighting on phone calls, nasty in their custody exchanges, and their friends constantly depressed. Is it possible to be peaceful in your divorce from your former spouse? Does it always have to be ugly? Is it possible to even be friendly to your ex? What can we learn to help us on the road to successful marriage?

The Answer: "We agree on the most important thing: you. We agree to co-parent because it is what's best for you. Dad and I love you too much to ever hate each other. Our choice to co-parent peacefully binds us together. Co-parenting peacefully is possible." Even for the couples who hurt the most. Start small. Love your babies and start today."

Tip # 27
Prioritize one-on-one time.

Sometimes the best way to help your new blended family is to spend time apart. Parents and children need time alone together without the new parent. The couple needs time alone together without the children. And the Blended Family parent and the child need some easy, low-key, one-on-one time together without the biological parent. This allows each person in the stepfamily to get what he or she needs from the other. Strengthening the individual bonds in the Blended family will help strengthen the family.

Tip # 28

Give permission.

Blended families can be bound up with guilt and insecurities and confusing, contrasting emotions. Release some of this tension by giving family members the freedom to feel, grieve, express, love, and act. Give permission to your spouse to spend guilt-free time with his or her biological children. Give your Blended family children permission not to like you. Give your children permission to like your ex's new spouse. Give yourself permission to care of yourself with exercise, time in nature, or an hour with a good friend.

Let relationships develop naturally, but also look to provide opportunities to help them do so. You can't force a child to like or love these new people that come into the family. You can find ways to gently nudge and encourage family members in that direction. Shared experiences, one-on-one time, and a life lived together will help to develop these bonds. The longing for blending is so understandable. Blended Families is a process, not an event.

Tip # 29
Expect bumps and adjust as needed.

Whether you are parenting Blended Family children or biological children, they change as they grow up and your parenting needs to adjust as well. Children also naturally act out to test the boundaries of a new family dynamic such as a Blended family. Children are feeling their way of how much control they have and may try to play both parents off each other or create tensions. Don't take this as a personal attack or a sign that your Blended family is doomed. Work with the ebb and flow of your Blended family.

Tip # 30

Seek Support

Consider searching out therapy, coaching, or other support groups to start your Blended family off on the right foot. Whether there is a divorce or a death, children from both spouses or from just one, no two Blended families have the same situation, dynamic, or pieces to fit together. Seeking professional counseling can allow an objective third party to help you navigate the waters of your specific situation. In family therapy sessions, everyone gets a chance to talk, everyone feels heard, and agreements can be made with the help of a neutral third party where everyone feels that they were in on the decision. That can help you create a recipe for Blended family success.

"Families don't have to match. You don't have to look like someone else to love them."

—LEIGH ANNE TUOHY

MOTHER OF MICHAEL OHER.

PROFILED IN *THE BLIND SIDE*

Tip # 31

As wonderful as it is to have found love the second time around, living in a blended family can seem particularly stressful at times. Newly formed families -- and experts say that **"new"** is a term that can apply for up to seven years, as everyone learns to navigate old loyalties, unfamiliar relationships, and developmental changes -- need lots of advice, and they know it. Conflict about how to handle children is tough on everyone and can be murder on a marriage. (It's one of the reasons second unions fail more than first ones.)
What do you do if you feel like one of your children is trying to come between you? How do you tell your spouse without sounding jealous? A lot of time they are just a little child longing for their parents, and if we're smart, we will encourage them. One of the biggest myths about blended families is that there should be a lot of

family togetherness, and there will be an instant sense of intimacy. Our children are likely just seeking the time and attention they were is used to getting from their parent. Don't worry – they are not plotting. Children can't grasp the intricacies of relationships (or how to bust them up) until around age 10. Before then, they're just normally egocentric. In blended families, we should strive to make sure the children get alone time with their mother or father, fun time with both of you, and one-on-one opportunities with you too.

Tip # 32

Creating a Family

Once you've put your parenting house in order, turning it into a loving, well-blended home is another task entirely. Blended families need time together in order to bond and figure out the new relationships, a tall order when you consider visitation and custody schedules.

But you don't have to carve out enormous blocks of time to connect with one another. Reading a story together every night before bed or taking a weekly trip to the playground as a family helps children feel loved and listened to, cornerstones of harmonious family life.

And because children in blended families may spend lots of time moving from house to house, establishing return rituals is another way to smooth the transition and show them you're not just Daddy's new wife -- you're also a caregiver. When we do a house switch, we always stop for ice cream on the way home. It gives us all some grace time before jumping into a different routine. It also turns a potentially anxiety-provoking transition into a fun family ritual the children eagerly look forward to.

Remember, too, that the most important relationship to nurture in any stepfamily is between the adult partners. In fact, putting more energy and effort into coupledom may improve your relationships with all the children, who will begin to see you as a strong, united front instead of two bewildered (or even squabbling) individuals. To accomplish this goal, you need to set aside time alone with your partner to discuss family issues. At each meeting, pick the two most important problems you've been having and brainstorm solutions. At the end of each meeting, do something special: Give each other backrubs, or watch a movie to reward yourselves. And schedule regular date nights and weekends away when children-related topics are off limits. All this planning, scheduling, and communicating is tough but worth it. We know that you need to work hard to make a happy marriage and family.

Tip # 33

The Ex Files

No matter how hard you work on household harmony within your own four walls, it's important that you do the same with ex-partners. Research shows that one of the primary sources of children's problems after a divorce is the inability of parents to keep their negative feelings about their ex (or their ex's new partner) to themselves. Remember, children take their emotional cues from their parents. Negative comments about what goes on in that other household just makes it harder on your children. In a perfect world, the rules and values in each of your child's homes would be identical. In the real world, the most practical way of handling inevitable household differences is to choose what's most important to you and compromise when necessary. Be the best parent you can be and give your ex the benefit of the doubt when you can. Of course, sometimes ex-partners are vested in keeping a fight going. Sometimes the mother of your children, has not gotten past the bitterness of her divorce. However, she may say, **"I really think it's best for our children if we can get along, so I just keep trying to be nice."** Most important is to keep your own home as peaceful and structured as possible, no matter how fierce a battle zone your ex tries to create.

Tip # 34

The Children Are All Right?

The most unpredictable part of the blended family equation may well be how the children deal with one another. The truth is, many children consider new siblings a nuisance or even a threat. Your 2-year-old may feel dethroned if she finds herself living with a cute 1-year-old brother, and your 4-year-old may resent the fact that his kindergartner new sister gets to color on the big-kid worksheets. Interestingly, one of the best strategies you can employ to make sure new siblings get along is to recognize that a blended family is a family within a family -- and that you and your children need your own time together. Respecting and cherishing your original family help children realize that they're still special and not just part of a bigger group. So, take off for the zoo with your 3-year-old, just the two of you. And let your partner do the same with his children.

As much as you want each child to feel special, you also want them all to feel they're getting equal treatment. This is often difficult, because multiple homes frequently mean multiple opportunities for gifts and activities. It's hard for a 3-year-old to see her new sister come home with a new Barbie from her grandma and not want one herself. According to experts, trying to even out these kinds of situations is a losing battle. It's impossible for everything to be equal in any household. The best way for you to handle this challenge is to be equal when you can be -- spend the same amount on each child for holiday gifts, for example, and stand firm on your decision to say no to an extra gift even if a new sibling gets one more from her mom.

Of course, adding a new baby to the blend creates a whole other set of child-related situations as family positions shift once again. As wonderful as a new baby is, there's no guarantee that the children will be thrilled by their arrival and embrace them immediately. For instance, if the children are younger than 5 and have felt neglected by their noncustodial parent or by a Blended parent, they may feel intense jealousy. But young children with good relationships with their parents and Blended parents will most likely react the same way all young children react to a new sibling: with a mixture of jealousy and affection.

Experts say that babies are good for your marriage; Blended parents who have not had children may find that adding a baby diminishes issues with children or ex-spouses because now they appreciate the parent-child bond firsthand. And regardless of how many children there are, or which parents are also Blended parents, a new arrival adds a unique intimacy to a family. A baby makes life more challenging, but new children seems to have brought everyone closer. He's a link between all of us.

In the end, the most comforting piece of advice about blending families is this: A blended family is a family, first and foremost. The more parenting experiences you gain, the more mistakes you make and learn from, the better you become at being a parent, Blended parent, and spouse. The result? A happier, well-adjusted, well-blended family.

Tip # 35

Statistics show that **"approximately one-third of all weddings in America today form Blended families."** A look at different types of Blended families can highlight the unique challenges each stepfamily may encounter.

Portrait no. 1: Husband with children marries never-married, no-children wife.

Dads who remarry often expect their new brides to assume a similar role to their former wife. The new wife, on the contrary, steps into the marriage ready for romance and quality time together as a couple. Instantly filling the role of wife is challenge enough; being interim Mom is often overwhelming. Wives in this situation often feel frustration and disillusionment when they are handed someone else's children to care for (and the children don't like it, either!).

In this scenario, Dad must step up to the plate and handle the disciplining of his children to avoid conflict with his new wife. He should also teach the children to treat their new mom with respect and talk through (or even write down) household duties with his new wife until a fair arrangement is reached.

Tip # 36

Portrait no. 2: Wife with children marries no-children husband.
Entering this marriage, Mom's relief at having a new partner in life might result in her handing off too many responsibilities to her new husband. The children, then, usually will rebel. They have a dad (or had one); they don't think they need a new one. Tread lightly with any Blended parent administering discipline. Biological parents are the ones who should handle rules and punishments, at least initially. This couple needs to bond and show solidarity to the children. The wife must be careful not to shut out her new husband in favor of her children. Avoid inside jokes with the children and subtle put-downs that would cause the children to disregard their new Blended father altogether. There is a fine line between handling the discipline and devaluing the husband's position in the home. Require children to show the same respect for their new dad that they would any teacher, law enforcement officer, or other adult in authority. Don't try to force love.

Tip # 37

Portrait no. 3: Divorced mom with children marries divorced dad with children.
This type of Blended family may seem to come with the most hurdles to overcome initially but has potential to be the most successful makeup because Mom and Dad are motivated to pull together for the children. Children, however, experience the most loss when their parent marries someone with children. Access to their biological parent must now be shared by not just the new spouse but also by other children. Their physical space is shared with a Blended parent and Blended siblings. New cities, new home, new school and new roommate are also common changes when families join. And, some children must face the end of their dream of their parents reuniting. The first two years in any Blended family, but especially this type, are

crucial. Expect conflict and extend grace — lots of it. There will be different relationships between members of this type of Blended family, different levels of intimacy, connection, and love between Blended siblings and between children and stepparents. Don't worry; that's normal.

Tip # 38

Portrait no. 4: Divorced or widowed parents of adult children marry.

Even if the children have left the nest, remarried couples with children still qualify as Blended families. Due to a lack of daily interactions, bonding and connecting may be more difficult. Many relationships will be strained for years or may never achieve any level of intimacy. Blended parents and Blended children can try to connect through cards, letters, phone calls, emails and family get-togethers.

Unique issues to this Blended family may include establishing healthy grandparenting relationships and inheritance tension. Family fears can be alleviated by communication and a welcoming love.

Distributing family keepsakes ahead of time or deciding how you will distribute your property can ease some of the tensions related to inheritance.

No matter what type of Blended family yours may fall under, with the right resources and the help of God, family, and friends, your Blended family can find encouragement and hope.

Tip # 39

"We're in love and we're ready to get married," they said. **"Terrific,"** we responded. **"Are your children ready for you to get married?"** It was the first session of pre-marital counseling and already Abdul and Kareema were caught off-guard. **"What do you mean?"** Kareema asked. **"I'm sure our children will have some adjustments to make, but that shouldn't take long. Besides, my children are really enjoying Mike at this point — what's to be concerned about?"** I could tell already that this couple was like most: They grossly underestimated the transition that remarriage has on the single-parent home. We had a lot of work to do.

My opening question was much different from Angie and Mike's. It had been five years since her divorce and she had made a concerted effort to work toward healing and create a stable home for her children. As a result, her home and children were functioning well, despite some financial pressures. She met Abdul about six months prior to our meeting and according to her it started out well.

"I finally met a friend I could trust and confide in, not to mention someone who made me feel cared for. I had been craving that for some time. But now things are starting to progress and I'm afraid to remarry — not because I'm afraid to commit again — but because I know Blended family life is very difficult and I don't want my children to suffer any more. What should I do?"

Kareema was keenly aware that most Blended families end in divorce and she didn't want to become another statistic or put her children through more heartache. She needed some answers.

As we conduct Blended family seminars around the country, the two most consistent questions I hear from single-parents are:

"Should I remarry?"

"When we get married, how do we help our children and family to succeed?"

We never tell couples whether they should remarry, but we do admonish them to Blend in a way from their remarriage fantasies and consider the realities of Blended family life. In order to make a Blended family the right direction for you and your children, you first must understand the challenges of Blended family living and then make an informed choice about remarriage.

Tip # 40
Blended family Challenges

Blended families are unique in many ways. Unfortunately, the **"Brady Bunch"** disguised most of those differences and gave America an artificial security about Blended family life. If you watched that show you probably assume Blended families are just like biological families.

Nothing could be further from the truth. Here are just a few factors for single parents to consider before stepping into a Blended family. Don't begin the journey unless you've done your homework, counted the cost and are willing to persevere until you reach the 'Promised Land. In the Old Testament of the Bible, when the Israelites realized they were trapped between Pharaoh's army and the Red Sea, they cried out in fear and anger to Moses wishing they had stayed in Egypt. Nearly every Blended family, shortly after remarriage, experiences a painful pinch between the losses and hurts of their past and the sea of opposition that stands in their future. Children are often heard crying, **"Mom, why did you marry this guy? We were so much better off when it was just us."** Truly, the journey to the Promised Land for most is not an easy one. But if you trust God and persevere, He will lead you through to better days.

Make sure you're not still haunted by the ghost of marriage past. Emotional and spiritual healing from divorce or the death of a spouse takes time; in fact, the average person requires three to five years before they can be discerning about a new relationship. Don't let the rebound-bug bite you where it hurts. After his wife died of cancer Idriss found himself lonely and feeling inadequate to care for his daughter. **"I guess I needed a partner and I wanted a mother for my child,"** he said. This emptiness led him to rush into a new marriage that ended after just one year. Remember, time is your best friend, so slow down the courting process.

Realize that a parent's relationship with his children will be an intimacy barrier to the new marriage. As we write this book, we think of all the couples we've seen over the years. One day, a Blended mother came to see me hoping I could help diminish the jealousy she feels toward her Blended son. Five years into the marriage and she still plays second fiddle. Yet the solution is not as simple as telling the biological parent, **"Just put your spouse first."** Biological parents can't just switch their loyalties; it feels like they're betraying their children. **"After all,"** said one mother, **"My children have suffered enough, and I don't want them to lose me, too."** Despite this struggle, the couple must learn to nurture their relationship and not get lost in the Blended family shuffle.

Understand that creating a Blended family takes time. Every Blended family has an assumed blending style (whether they know it or not) that drives how they treat one another. For example, a food processor mentality results in parents demanding that Blended children call their Blended parent **"Dad"** or **"Mom"** right away. In effect, the noncustodial biological parent gets chopped up in the process. A pressure cooker mentality is used when new family members are forced into spending time together. Usually the lid blows off the pot. And finally, the blender mentality assumes that everyone will love everyone else to the same degree. Not only does this set people up for conflict it usually results in someone being creamed. Instead, develop a Crock-Pot mentality that allows for time (the average blended family requires seven years to combine) and low heat to bring the various members of the family into relationship. For example, instead of forcing the family together, Jarvis and Julie spent Saturday afternoons each with their own children. Only after nearly two years did they begin to combine leisure activities. This low-heat approach didn't threaten the children's relationship with their parents and made space for new relationships to develop.

Accept the fact that remarriage is a gain for the adults and a loss for the children. What they really want is for Mom and Dad to reunite, so for them the remarriage is a loss. When you add that to the list of hundreds of other losses, they've already experienced you can see why children have mixed feelings about the new family. Furthermore, loss always brings the fear of more loss. When persons start protecting themselves from more loss, walls are built. **"I'm afraid my children and new husband will turn against each other. It would be just another failure,"** said one mom. Her teenage son echoed her fear, **"I'm afraid of getting close to anyone. With all I've had to live through I keep waiting for it to happen all over again."**

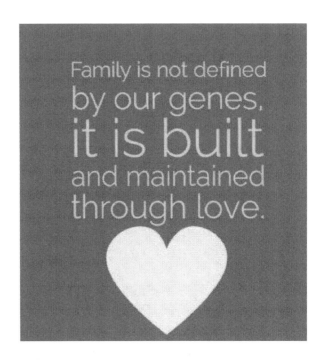

Family is not defined by our genes, it is built and maintained through love.

Tip # 41

Courting is important but true blended family relationships start with the wedding. Children are sometimes tolerant, even encouraging of their parent's new romance, but they frequently change their tune when real Blended family life begins. Daran called us the day after he and Gabina married. After dating for two years, they spent three months in pre-marital counseling with us trying to work through issues from the past and anticipating the needs of their children. Even though much had been accomplished, on the day of the wedding, Gabina's 16- and 19-year-old daughters began badgering their mother. They had appeared supportive of her decision, but now that Daran was really moving in, they berated Gabina over her decision to divorce their father and remarry. Gabina spent her wedding night in tears.

Discuss and develop a plan for your parenting roles. For the first couple of years after remarriage, it's generally best for the biological parent to remain the main source of nurturance, affection and discipline. The Blended parent's role may evolve from a "babysitter" role (where they borrow power from the biological parent and enforce "their" rules), to an "uncle or aunt" (where the children consider the Blended parent extended family, but not a parent), to a "parental role model" with a considerable measure of authority. This gradual progression gives the Blended parent and Blended children time and space to develop a relationship before power battles come into play.

Tip # 42

Develop a working relationship with your ex-spouse. Daana thought her negative relationship with her ex-husband could never change. She learned, however, that seeking to forgive him and avoiding pushing his hot buttons helped to diminish their negative interaction. Gradually their co-parenting relationship improved, and their children became more cooperative in each household. This in turn opened the door for Daana's new husband to interact with her children and gradually build a relationship.
Loyalties, left unattended, will divide and conquer a Blended family. Allow children to love both biological parents and don't force a relationship with the Blended parent(s). Let children set the pace for their new Blended-relationships and don't worry if they aren't **"warming up"** as quickly as you'd like. Naim worked very hard to win the heart of his 12-year-old new daughter. But after only four months he gave up because she didn't seem to be returning any of the effort. With a Crock-Pot mentality Naim would have understood that relationship building takes years, not months.

Tip # 43

Consider the potential for sexual pressures within the home. The incidence of Blended family incest is eight times greater than in biological families. Blended siblings are often confronted with sexual thoughts that lead to shame or inappropriate behavior. Patman and his wife of 10 years approached us at a recent seminar after her 13-year-old son admitted to sneaking into his 14-year-old Blended sister's room to fondle her. They had been living in the same house for 10 years, yet the lack of blood relations left the door open for abuse. Sexual indiscretions in Blended families are real and must be guarded against. Attempts have been made to describe motivational categories of incest. The categories for incest that you must guard against are the following:

• Affection-based: the incest provides closeness in a family otherwise lacking in nurture and affection. There is an emphasis on the specialness of the relationship, within which otherwise unavailable caring is given and received.

• Erotic-based: the family atmosphere is one of chaotic pansexuality, and it is not uncommon for many members to be involved. Its norm is the erotization of relationships. The term "polyincest" is often used to describe such multiple-perpetrator situations.

• Aggression-based: the incestuous acts involve the perpetrator's sexualized anger. The perpetrator vents his or her frustration and conflicts on a vulnerable individual, and physical mistreatment is often involved.

• Rage-based: the perpetrator is hostile and may be overtly sadistic. There may be great danger to the victim.

It is not unusual for mixtures of these components to be encountered. Many do not think that interactions without actual sexual events should be called incest. When a parent uses a child to serve the parent's emotional needs and promotes a child to a special and close role, however, that child becomes a surrogate spouse, trapped in a world dominated by the needs of a parent. This type of relationship, which is often simultaneously seductive and critical, is often called "emotional incest."

Tip # 44

Making the Decision to Step Forward

Because Blended family life presents these and other challenges, it's important to invest in pre-marital counseling. Be sure to find a good Therapist or Student Minister who understands Blended family peculiarities. Unfortunately, this can be very difficult as clergy are just now beginning to wake up to the needs of Blended families, and most counselors don't have much Blended family training either. If a qualified counselor is not available in your area, you have purchased this book or attend one of our seminars for Blended families. Make sure you look in every direction before you leap, otherwise you might spend a lot of time wandering around the wilderness.

Blended family life is not impossible. Indeed, there is a 'Promised Land' of marital fulfillment, family stability and shared spirituality. But for most Blended families finding these rewards requires intentional effort and a keen understanding of how Blended families work best. After a lot of exploration, Huraiya and Hiram decided that remarriage was workable for their two families. And they were willing to accept the risks. Four years into the marriage the couple reports managing their initial adjustments well. Recently, however, Hiram's 15-year-old son unexpectedly decided to come live with them. New challenges are now confronting them, but they are seeking help from a local support group.

Waheedah has decided to focus her energies on her children. She explained to her Court mate that at this time things were not going to work out with him. But for now, not complicating her single-parent family with a remarriage seems best. His willingness to wait remains to be seen.

Tip # 45

Solid marriage

Without the marriage, there is no family. It's harder to take care of the marriage in a blended family because you don't have couple time like most first marriages do. You'll have to grow and mature into the marriage while parenting. Make this time a priority! If family members can be civil with one another on a regular basis rather than ignoring, purposely trying to hurt, or completely withdrawing from each other, they're on track.

All relationships are respectful. This is not just referring to the children's' behavior toward the adults. Respect should be given not just based on age, but also since you are all family members now. Compassion for everyone's development. Members of your blended family may be at various life stages and have different needs (teens versus toddlers, for example). They may also be at different stages in accepting this new family. Family members need to understand and honor those differences.

Room for growth. After a few years of being blended, hopefully the family will grow, and members will choose to spend more time together and feel closer to one another.

To give yourself the best chance of success in creating a blended family, it's important to start planning how the new family will function before the marriage even takes place.

Tip # 46

Planning your blended family

Having survived a painful divorce or separation and then managed to find a new loving relationship, the temptation can often be to rush into remarriage and a blended family without first laying solid foundations. By taking your time, you give everyone a chance to get used to each other and used to the idea of marriage.

Too many changes at once can unsettle children. Blended families have the highest success rate if the couple waits two years or more after a divorce to remarry, instead of piling one drastic family change onto another.

Don't expect to fall in love with your partner's children overnight. Get to know them. Love and affection take time to develop.

Find ways to experience **"real life"** together. Taking both sets of children to a theme park every time you get together is a lot of fun, but it isn't reflective of everyday life. Try to get the children used to your partner and their children in daily life situations.

Make parenting changes before you marry. Agree with your new partner how you intend to parent together, and then make any necessary adjustments to your parenting styles before you remarry. It'll make for a smoother transition and your children won't become angry at your new spouse for initiating changes.

Tip # 47

Don't allow ultimatums

Your children or new partner may put you in a situation where you feel you must choose between them. Remind them that you want both sets of people in your life.

Insist on respect. You can't insist people like each other, but you can insist that they treat one another with respect.

Limit your expectations. You may give a lot of time, energy, love, and affection to your new partner's children that will not be returned immediately. Think of it as making small investments that may one day yield a lot of interest.

Given the right support, children should gradually adjust to the prospect of marriage and being part of a new family. It is your job to communicate openly, meet their needs for security, and give them plenty of time to make a successful transition.

Tip # 48

Bonding with your new blended family

You will increase your chances of successfully bonding with your new Blended children by thinking about what they need. Age, gender, and personality are not irrelevant, but all children have some basic needs and wants that once met can help you establish a rewarding new relationship.

Children want to feel:

Safe and secure. Children want to be able to count on parents and Blended parents. Children of divorce have already felt the upset of having people they trust let them down and may not be eager to give second chances to a new blended parent.

Loved. Children like to see and feel your affection, although it should be a gradual process.

Valued. Children often feel unimportant or invisible when it comes to decision making in the new blended family. Recognize their role in the family when you make decisions.

Heard and emotionally connected. Creating an honest and open environment free of judgment will help children feel heard and emotionally connected to a new Blended parent. Show them that you can view the situation from their perspective.

Appreciated and encouraged. Children of all ages respond to praise and encouragement and like to feel appreciated.

Limits and boundaries. Children may not think they need limits, but a lack of boundaries sends a signal that the child is unworthy of the parents' time, care, and attention. As a new Blended parent, you shouldn't step in as the enforcer at first, but work with your spouse to set limits.

Tip # 49

Let your Blended child set the pace
Every child is different and will show you how slow or fast to go as you get to know them. Some children may be more open and willing to engage. Shy, introverted children may require you to slow down

and give them more time to warm up to you. The cardinal rule for building a relationship with a Blended child is this; let the child set the pace. Gauge their level of openness to you and match it. If they jump into your lap or want to give you a hug don't leave them hanging. But if they bristle when you try to hug them back up a bit and find something less intimidating. Just remember, letting the child set the pace is just how you start. It will grow well beyond that over time. Given enough time, patience, and interest, most children will eventually give you a chance.

Tip # 50

Use routines and rituals to bond

As well as building relationships, the early months are also about establishing your new blended family and the way you live together. This might include: working out **new family routines** and household responsibilities – for example, who cooks dinner, makes the children's lunches, or does the shopping and cleaning. They also might include setting up **new family rules and** sorting out bedrooms and work or study spaces for the children.

New and old rituals can help as you work out how your blended family will live together. Rituals can give family members a sense of belonging and can help comfort children in unfamiliar circumstances. Your rituals might be a mix of those that you and your partner already have, or you can think of new ones for your family. For example, if your child loves listening to you read a bedtime story, carrying on that tradition will help him feel comfortable in your new family. Or you could think about weekly rituals for the whole family, like playing board games on a Sunday.

Creating family routines and rituals can help you bond with your new children and unite the family. Plan to incorporate at least one new family ritual, such as Sunday visits to the Mosque and maybe even to a beach, or special ways to celebrate a family birthday. Establishing regular family meals, for example, offers a great chance for you to talk and bond with your children and new children as well as encourage healthy eating habits.

© Can Stock Photo

Tip # 51

Dealing with the death of a parent

When a parent has died, the remarriage of the remaining parent may trigger unfinished grieving in children. Give them space and time to grieve. Here are other suggestions for you:

Listen

Allowing your children to freely share their thoughts and feelings. This will help them through the grieving process and encouraged their acceptance of you. Let them know that while you are in the position of their mother or father, you are not taking their place in the home.

Be patient

Sometimes the children will make comparisons between you and their deceased parent. These comparisons are very hard not to take personally. While it is tempting to do (but not necessary) try to remind yourself of your new blended family son or daughters outstanding qualities and continue to act to bring them out.

Remember

Let your new children determine how they want to mark important dates to them such as Mothers or Father's Day and her Mother or Fathers birthday and date of death. It varied from year to year. Sometimes you can donate in hopes of a cure to an Organization; other times we placed a rose on our table. Use whatever occasion you can to honor your new children's memory of their deceased parent. Being a Blended parent to a child whose natural parent has died will teach you how to have grace and class with your children.

Tip # 52

Helping children adjust

Children of different ages and genders tend to adjust differently to a blended family. The physical and emotional needs of a two-year-old girl are different than those of a 13-year-old boy, but don't mistake differences in development and age for differences in fundamental needs. Just because a teenager may take a long time accepting your love and affection doesn't mean that he doesn't want it. You will need to adjust your approach with different age levels and genders, but your goal of establishing a trusting relationship is the same.

Young children under 10

May adjust more easily because they thrive on cohesive family relationships.

Are more accepting of a new adult.

Feel competitive for their parent's attention.

Have more daily needs to be met.

Adolescents aged 10-14

May have the most difficult time adjusting to a Blended family.

Need more time to bond before accepting a new person as a disciplinarian.

May not demonstrate their feelings openly but may be even more sensitive than young children when it comes to needing love, support, discipline and attention.

Teenagers 15 or older

May have less involvement in Blended Family life.

Prefer to separate from the family as they form, their own identities.

May not be open in their expression of affection or sensitivity, but still want to feel important, loved and secure.

Gender Differences – general tendencies:

Both boys and girls in Blended families tend to prefer verbal affection, such as praises or compliments, rather than physical closeness, like hugs and kisses.

Girls tend to be uncomfortable with physical displays of affection from their Blended father.

Boys seem to accept a Blended father more quickly than girls.

Attachment relationships and blended families

Anyone with an insecure attachment history may have problems establishing close, loving bonds with new members of a blended family. Fortunately, an insecurely attached child (or adult) can learn to trust and bond with others.

Tip # 53

Common challenges

As you blend two families, differences in parenting, discipline, lifestyle, etc., can create challenges and become a source of frustration for the children. Agreeing on consistent guidelines about rules, chores, discipline, and allowances will show the children that you and your spouse intend to deal with issues in a similar and fair way.

Other common challenges include:

Age differences. In blended families, there may be children with birthdays closer to one another than possible with natural siblings, or the new Blended parent may be only a few years older than the eldest child.

Parental inexperience. One Blended parent may have never been a parent before, and therefore may have no experience of the different stage's children go through.

Changes in family relationships. If both parents remarry partners with existing families, it can mean children suddenly find themselves with different roles in two blended families. For example, one child may be the eldest in one blended family, but the youngest in the other. Blending families may also mean one child loses their uniqueness as the only boy or girl in the family.

Difficulty in accepting a new parent. If children have spent a long time in a one-parent family, or still nurture hopes of reconciling their parents, it may be difficult for them to accept a new person.

Coping with demands of others. In blended families, planning family events can get complicated, especially when there are custody considerations to consider. Children may grow frustrated that vacations, parties, or weekend trips now require complicated arrangements to include their new Blended siblings.

Changes in family traditions. Most families have very different ideas about how annual events such as holidays, birthdays, and family vacations should be spent. Children may feel resentful if they're forced to go along with someone else's routine. Try to find some common ground or create new traditions for your blended family.

Parental insecurities. A new parent may be anxious about how they compare to a child's natural parent or may grow resentful if the children compare them unfavorably to the natural parent.

Tip # 54

Strengthening your blended family

Establishing trust is crucial to creating a strong, cohesive blended family. At first, children may feel uncertain about their new family and resist your efforts to get to know them. This is often simply apprehension about having to share their parent with a new spouse (and Blended siblings). Try not to take their negative attitudes personally. Instead, build trust and strengthen your new blended family by:

Creating clear boundaries

Discuss the role each Blended parent will play in raising their respective children, as well as changes in household rules.

Establish the Blended parent as more of a friend or counselor rather than a disciplinarian.

Let the biological parent remain primarily responsible for discipline until the Blended parent has developed solid bonds with the children.

Create a list of family rules. Discuss the rules with the children and post them in a prominent place. Understand what the rules and boundaries are for the children in their other residence, and, if possible, be consistent.

Tip # 55

Keeping ALL parents involved

Children will adjust better to the blended family if they have access to both biological parents. It is important if all parents are involved and work toward a parenting partnership.

Let the children know that you and your ex-spouse will continue to love them and be there for them throughout their lives.

Tell the children that your new spouse will not be a 'replacement' mom or dad, but another person to love and support them.

Tip # 56

Communicating often and openly

The way a blended family communicates says a lot about the level of trust between family members. When communication is clear, open, and frequent, there are fewer opportunities for misunderstanding and more possibilities for connection, whether it is between parent and child, Blended parent and Blended child, or between Blended siblings.

Discuss everything. Uncertainty and worry about family issues comes from poor communication, so talk as much as possible.

Never keep emotions bottled up or hold grudges and try to address conflict positively.

Listen respectfully to one another. Establish an open and nonjudgmental atmosphere.

Provide opportunities for communication by doing things together as a family—games, sports, activities.

Tip # 57

Tips for a healthy Blended family

All brothers and sisters **"fall out,"** so don't assume all family arguments are the result of living in a blended family.

Beware of favoritism. Be fair. Don't overcompensate by favoring your Blended children. This is a common mistake, made with best intentions, to avoid indulging your biological children.

Make special arrangements. If some of the children "just visit," make sure they have a locked cupboard for their personal things. Bringing toothbrushes and other things each time they come to your home makes them feel like a visitor, not a member of the blended family.

Find support. Locate a Blended parenting support organization in your community. You can learn how other blended families overcome challenges.

Spend time every day with your child. Try to spend at least one **"quiet time"** period with your child daily. Even in the best of blended families, children still need to enjoy some **"alone time"** with each parent.

Tip # 58

Maintaining marriage quality in a blended family

While newly remarried couples without children can use their first months together to build on their relationship, couples in a blended family are often more consumed with their children than each other. But focusing on building a strong marital bond will ultimately benefit everyone, including the children. If children see love, respect, and open communication between you and your spouse, they will feel more secure and are more likely to model those qualities.

Set aside time as a couple by making regular dates or meeting for lunch or coffee during school time.

Present a unified parenting approach to the children—arguing or disagreeing in front of them may encourage them to try to come between you.

Tip # 59

When to seek help

If, despite all your best efforts, your new spouse and/or children are not getting along, find a way to protect and nurture the children. It might be time to seek **outside help from a therapist, counselor or Student Minister** if:

(1) a child directs anger upon a family member or openly resents a Blended parent or their natural parent
(2) a Blended parent or natural parent openly favors one child over another
(3) members of the family derive no pleasure from usually enjoyable activities such as school, working, playing, or being with friends and family

Tip # 60

We all have heard the stats pertaining to the **divorce** rate of marriages in the American home. Although the precise number varies depending on your source, you will find that the numbers hover around 42 to 49% for the first **marriage** then escalates to around 60 to 67% for the second marriage then jumps again to approximately 74% for marriage number three. We'll stop there in the interest of brevity, but there is obviously a trending north of 75% for nuptials four and higher.

Hopefully those of us who have divorced more than once have at some point taken an inward journey to assess where the challenges in our decisions stem. This is certainly not an indictment or a judgment call from anyone. Have you really assessed why you got divorced in the first place?

Tip # 61

All human beings want to feel loved and they belong to someone or something. This family becomes that unit of **love** and belonging despite the current of external influences.

Made a vow that you would never treat your spouse in a manner that you would not want to be treated. Sound familiar? We've made that Golden Rule more relevant on a micro level by adapting the following.

(1) Make eating dinner together as a family non-negotiable. Try eating dinner together as a family with the television turned off.

(2) We've learned to accept each other as individuals without trying to change them, the same way we will have to accept people in the world outside our home.

(3) If change is necessary, we discuss the issue with a clear and concise explanation of its benefits as well as the penalty for non-compliance both in our home and in life.

(4) We take the time to learn each other and appreciate the strengths and challenges we all inherently have and discuss them in a loving and non-judgmental atmosphere.

(5) We make appropriate family decisions together so therefore all parties have a stake in the process and outcome.

(6) Spouses must vow to keep major disagreements away from the children with the **understanding** that we explain that

mom and dad do disagree without having to be disagreeable or create a contentious atmosphere.

(7) We tend to keep short accounts with each other and not let issues build up in layers thus causing a volcanic explosion.

(8) We teach our children and each other the type of things that one should easily **forgive** and let go versus the issues that should be dealt with directly and promptly.

(9) We bind together and multiply each other's joys and accomplishments so that we can also divide each other's failings and sorrows.

(10) We start and maintain family traditions such as saying I love you at least three times a day and making birthdays and other occasions special. We even make up our own holidays that we keep sacred in our home.

(11) We say grace over every meal and even publicly we bow our head in prayer. We believe that if we teach our children that it is okay to display their belief system publicly then they will seldom be ashamed of who they are.

Certainly, there is no magic to successfully raising a blended family. Your children will benefit from your legacy you've created filled with fond thoughts and **memories**. We are only sharing with you tips to creating a beautiful blended family. You must try in this day and time to do it.

Tip # 62

Emotional attachment, trust, and love are what open the door to influence in parenting. Once that is established, an adult—foster parent, grandparent, adoptive parent, or Blended parent—can lead and discipline a child. Said another way, the adage is true: Rules without relationship leads to rebellion. Wise new parents understand this and grow relationship in order to grow authority.

Authority can exist without a bonded relationship, but it has its limits. A police officer can pull you over, a boss or coach can tell you what to do, and a teacher can tell a student the rules of the classroom, but none of these authorities obtain obedience out of love or deep admiration.

Until Blended parents establish a love-relationship with a child, they are just external authorities imposing boundaries. That's why it's critical early in a blended family that stepparents recognize these limits and borrow power from the biological parent. If they limit their role, they can sabotage the developing relationships and any authority they might have had along with it. Therefore, for new parents the question is: How do they establish themselves as authority figures while waiting for bonding to occur?

Borrowing power

Think about babysitters. On their first visit to a home, they don't have any relational authority with children. The children don't know them, don't like them, and don't need them. But if the children and babysitter get many evenings together, they can form a significant relationship bond over time. In the meantime, while babysitters are hoping for a relationship to develop, how do they manage the children? Answer: by borrowing power.

Babysitters can put children in time-out, take away privileges, and declare bedtime because the child's parent has passed power to the babysitter. The "she's in charge while we're gone" speech is usually quite effective. Now notice, this empowers the babysitter to set boundaries and impose consequences that ultimately are owned by the parent. However, if the biological parent is unwilling or unable to own these boundaries, there will be chaos.

Blended parenting follows a similar process. Initially new parents act as extensions of the biological parent. They can enforce consequences, set boundaries, and say "no," but do so knowing full well they are not standing on their own authority. They live on borrowed power until such time as their love-relationship with the child matures and opens the door to more influence and authority.

Tip # 63

Discipline do's and don'ts for Blended parents

At best, new Blended parent authority is fragile and easily shattered. That's why these do's and don'ts must be a priority.

Do make sure the biological parent has your back. Biological parents must communicate to their children an expectation of obedience to the new parent and be willing to back up the new parent's actions. When disagreements occur, settle them in private.

Do strive for unity in parenting. Discuss behavioral expectations, boundaries, consequences, and values. Bring your parenting philosophies in line with each other. Don't be harsh or punish in a way that is inconsistent with the biological parent.

Do focus on relationship building. This is your long-term strength. Don't unilaterally change rules or try to make up for past parental mistakes or failings. Do listen to the child. If they draw into you sooner than expected, don't look back. Use the relational authority offered you. Don't get impatient. It often takes years to bond and develop a trusting love-relationship with children. Be persistent in bonding with them. Do communicate with the biological parent a lot! If uncertain, find parental unity before engaging the children.

Tip # 64

Taking action

Play! Having fun is a great way to connect. Do something fun.

Track with them. Know what activities a child is engaged in and enter that world. Take them to practice, ask about an activity, be aware of their world.

Take interest in the child's interests.

Share your talents, skills, and hobbies.

Communicate your commitment. Let the child know you value and want a relationship with them. This helps them to know your heart.

Share your spiritual walk. Shared spirituality can facilitate connection and a sense of family identity. Don't be preachy. Instead, share with humility your faith journey so they will see you as a safe person.

Tip # 65

Blended parenting is a delicate balancing act. Knowing when to Blend in or back away is challenging; missteps often pit biological parents and Blended parents against one another. The more abreast you are of Blended family dynamics, the better prepared you will be to help couples get on the same page and unify their family. Finding the right balance of authority and love is difficult with any child, but when that child is not your own, you really must think. Being united with your spouse about the boundaries for the children is crucial, as is consistency. But, even having said that, your relationship with the child is paramount, particularly in the early stages of living together as a blended family. This book should be helping you greatly.

Tip # 66

Things can get very difficult very quickly in a blended family. How can you discipline your new Blended Family children effectively and get their respect? Ofttimes, the Blended relationship is the barometer of how (or if) the family is coming together—and the child is the one who will determine that because you can't make anyone like you. It can be extremely hard to find the right balance when you're a new parent. Many adults try to blend their families with high expectations: they may think it will be like their first marriage in terms of time spent with their spouse and the attention they'll be able to give the relationship. Unfortunately, this couldn't be further from the truth. We like to say that first marriages are **"apples,"** and second marriages are **"oranges"**: you can't compare the two, because while a first marriage is all about your new partner, a subsequent marriage revolves around the children—and making sure that everyone has a place in the family. In working with Blended families over the years, we've found if the parents try to rush it or **"force a new family,"** it's not going to work out well. And here's the tough part for adults: the Blended relationship is the barometer of how (or if) the family is coming together—and the child is the one who will determine that, because you can't make anyone like you.

It's important to realize that everyone's role shifts when you create a Blended family. In fact, when you first bring everyone together, all the children will try to figure out where—or even if—they belong in the new system. If they don't believe they have a place—or if they think someone is taking their place—they'll often act out.

Tip # 67
Defer to the Bio-Parent

Surprised? It's true. As a Blended parent, it's important to defer to the bio-parent. Even though this might go against everything you expected, the new relationship needs time to develop. It's important not to be the heavy, but you can't disappear either. Maintaining your presence and at the same time supporting the bio-parent is difficult but will be productive. The irony is that when you relax and support the bio-parent, the relationship with your Blended child will form faster.

You're the good cop; let the bio-parent be the bad cop. If there's a behavior for which your new child needs a consequence, let your spouse deal with it and support their decision. The good cop finds out the interests of the new child and develops the relationship by getting involved in the child's life based on those discoveries.

Tip # 68
Don't Compete with Your Counterpart

Don't compete with your counterpart; rather, uphold them. In other words, don't try to be a better mom than your Blended Families bio-mom, or a better dad than their bio-dad. No matter what you think of the bio-parent's style of discipline (or lack thereof) it's important to respect and acknowledge the strength of the biological connection. This can be difficult to do when your new spouse is still at war with his or her ex, and possibly still fighting over the children and other issues.

Many Blended moms decide they're going to make up for all the hurt and pain. Many Blended fathers have an attitude of **"I'm going to shape up this platoon and lead the troops out of the wilderness."** But as somebody once said, **"If the Blended dad is leading and no one is following, he's just out for a walk."** We encourage Blended parents to establish a relationship with their Blended children rather than being a dictator or rigid authoritarian. Simply be present in the child's life and avoid **"fixing things"** or competing with the bio-parent.

Tip # 69

Discover Your Blended Child's Interests
Discover the things your new son or new daughter likes. Start off as you would with any friendship: find some common ground and do things together that you might both enjoy. Remember, you're just there to build a relationship appropriately, not to parent or take the place of your new child's mother or father. Come in as a friend or a benevolent aunt or uncle; in other words, choose a role other than "parent" in order to foster the relationship.

Tip # 70

Get Out of the Way
Let your spouse have one-on-one time with his or her children—without you. This helps reduce the displacement and loss the child might be feeling and assures him that he hasn't been displaced by somebody else. This flies in the face of the myth of "instant family." Encouraged their biological parent to do things with their children like go off for the weekend or do special things together. It will help everyone immeasurably. In all blended families, this reassures the children that they still belong and haven't lost the love of their bio-parent to the new spouse.
One of the most common complaints of biological parents is that they believe they're caught in the middle. We often hear, **"I love my spouse and I love my children, but I feel like I'm being pulled apart."** Many Blended parents get all sick and nervous if their spouse is still spending time with his or her children and not including them. Our advice to them is, **"Well, if you plan to be in this marriage awhile,**

don't worry about it—you'll get your turn." In the meantime, this relieves the bio-parent and releases them to enjoy their children— and lets the new children know you're not there to take their parent away.

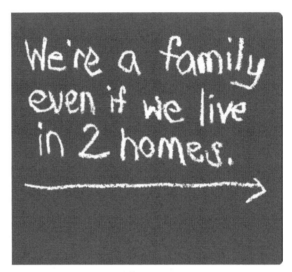

We're a family even if we live in 2 homes.

Tip # 71

Act Lovingly Even If You Don't Like Your Blended Family Children

We hear this all the time: **"I feel guilty because I don't love my blended children."** The reality is that you may never love them as your own—or even like them. And remember, you can't make your Blended Children like you, either! You are the **"intruder."** In their minds, you've displaced them. But even if you don't like them, you can learn to act lovingly toward them. Love is an action; so, behave in a loving manner toward your new children. It may surprise you down the road; as the relationship develops, love just may develop!

It's important to realize that because of the pain children experience after divorce—and continue to feel with a remarriage—they may act out. They may not have the skills to talk it out and express what's really going on inside. Many couples will come in for counseling and say, **"Fix these children."** Yet the children aren't broken—the family is. So, we ask the adults if they are willing to acknowledge the pain and brokenness that they created. If the couple can gain the skills to listen and understand what the child is going through, over time, the children will usually respond productively.

Tip # 72
Find Something Right

Find something good about your new children. Instead of focusing on the negative or complaining about them, find something positive to say to your spouse. That gets your husband or wife out of the middle and puts you in a more positive frame of mind about the children. Here's the analogy we like to use with the blended parents we see: The Blended family relationship is a **"baby relationship"**: it's brand new and very weak. It's like you're trying to pull a Mack truck with a piece of string. And if you pull too hard or discipline too rigidly, you'll just pop the string. So, take the time to develop the relationship, making the string into a cord, the cord into a rope, and the rope into a chain. The chain you end up with some day will be strong enough to take all the pushes and pulls of normal relationships. Be mindful that we are talking about years—not days, weeks, or months!

Tip # 73

About 75 percent of the 1.2 million Americans who **divorce** each year eventually remarry. Most have children, and, they find that Blended family life is more complex than they ever imagined. It's rife with complicated schedules, squabbling blended siblings, issues with ex-partners, and new spouses who've never been parents trying out childcare. Yet the flip side of life as a blended family is that there are many opportunities for joyful interactions. Most Blended parents genuinely grow to feel affection for the children in their care, and the children usually learn to accept and return the affection. And because you must work hard in a blended family to build relationships, it often ends up that everyone learns a lot about trust, safety, and love. When you become a Blended Family, your child-rearing role will be entirely different. Children who viewed you as a playmate may have trouble swallowing your discipline. Or, antics your partner found amusing on weekend visits with your toddler may lose their charm once you're all living together. One woman said, **"When I fell in love with my husband, I also fell for his 2-year-old daughter. At first, I was a glamorous babysitter, but once we were married, the glamour quickly rubbed off."**

One of her biggest surprises was that Brad was hesitant to discipline his daughter. When it came to their child's wants, their father couldn't say no, and that made his wife mad, especially when he let her sleep with them all the time. That's when she realized that if she wanted her new family to work, she'd have to shed her glorified babysitter role and act more like a parent. In order to make the Blended family transition smoothly, it's vital that you and your spouse sit down and hash out your child-rearing and discipline expectations. Children need parental consistency, or they become confused and insecure. It's little wonder, one of the greatest sources of tension in Blended families is dealing with discipline. Research shows that young children learn trust when they experience fair, effective discipline. Disagreements between parents about discipline often invite manipulation from the children, who quickly learn to pit adults against one another to get what they want.

Experts suggest that you and your partner develop a list of values you both want to teach, such as responsibility and honesty. Then tackle your beliefs on parenting. For example, you may think that time-out is an effective discipline tool, while your partner may feel it's a wimpy way out. Next, draft a list of household rules, such as how much TV the children can watch. Once you're both clear on each other's opinions, you can discuss discipline problems and what strategies you can use that will be effective for your family and that honor everyone's beliefs. That strategy worked for Cailee. She and her husband brainstormed together to find the perfect way to get Cailee to sleep on her own.

They decided to put a **'fairy tree'** in her room. Every time she spent the whole night in her room, they gave her a fairy to hang on it. After only 12 fairies, they had their bed to themselves again.

Of course, developing a strategy seems like child's play compared with following it, and it can be particularly difficult for a new Blended parent to start laying down the law. Early on, the children's biological parents should take responsibility for enforcing rules whenever possible, with the Blended parent acting as deputy.

Tip # 74

Due to issues such as differing parenting and discipline styles, the development of new relationships, and strong and potentially conflicting **emotions** from all sides, it may take time for one family to get used to living with the other family, even if they all got along before the families began living under the same roof. The couple may face difficulties adjusting to their new roles as part of a larger family, rather than just as a couple, and issues that arise with a partner's children may place **tension** on their newly formed bond. Individuals who do not have children of their own and are thus becoming parents for the first time when they enter the Blended parent role, might face additional stress as they become accustomed to the new role along with a new marriage. They may struggle to find the right balance between winning the affection and love of the children and parenting them appropriately, and it may take time to adjust to parenthood and be welcomed by a partner's children.

Tip # 75

Challenges Children Face
Children, especially older children, can easily become stressed by change, particularly when multiple changes occur at once. Children are often the ones most affected by the blending of a family: After children have experienced the divorce of their parents, they may find it difficult to adjust to a new parent and that parent's new rules, and they might express their frustration with behavioral or emotional outbursts.
Some children may also struggle with feelings for the new parent: Before the blending, a child may view a parent's significant other as a friend, but when the significant other becomes a parent, the child may resent what he or she views as a **"replacement"** of his or her other parent. Children might also be reluctant to **trust** a Blended

parent, especially those who may feel **abandoned** by a biological parent following a divorce. Further, when the child comes to care for the Blended parent, he or she may struggle with the new emotions, as the child may feel that **love** for the Blended parent somehow betrays his or her biological parent.

Sibling rivalry can also take on a new dimension, as children may feel compelled to compete for attention and dominance in the new household. A child may also worry that his or her biological parents may come to prefer the child's Blended siblings.

Tip # 76

Visitations with the other parent can also present difficulties. What was once the **"normal"** routine—one family spending unscheduled and unstructured time together every day, planning events in a flexible or spontaneous manner—gives way to what can be a confusing, insecure pattern, where scheduling conflicts create tension, and new family members may find it difficult to find the time to get used to one another. In addition, children may complain about the Blended parent to the **"outside"** parent, which can strain relations in what may already be a tense relationship.

Grief can also be a factor in the transition. When a remarriage takes place following the death of one parent, a child may still be **grieving** the loss of the other parent and could be further triggered by the remarriage. Children in these situations will often need more space and time to finish the grieving process before they can come to accept the new parent.

Tip # 77

Adults who are planning to remarry or cohabitate with children from previous relationships might wish to plan and prepare to face challenges by talking with one another and with their children about any possible differences in **parenting styles** and positive ways to handle any conflicts that might arise. When parenting changes take place before the actual marriage, the transition to living together will often go more smoothly.

Praise, encouragement, and demonstrated affection may all help ease the concerns of children who are reluctant to trust a Blended parent or who are worried that a biological parent might come to love them less. Parents may also wish to reassure their children that they will answer any questions and discuss any feelings the children might have.

Some families may also find it beneficial to attend therapy as a family. Counseling both before a remarriage that will result in a blended family and during the transition process may help ease the tensions that often arise in newly blended families.

Tip # 78

Family therapy is often an effective way for a blended family to work through the issues that each member brings to the new family. Family members can expect to attend most sessions as a group, though the therapist may also schedule separate, supplemental sessions with each child and with one or both parents. There are many approaches to family counseling, though most are linked to **family systems therapy**, which views the family as a system and each member's role as being directly informed by the functioning of the family system. Other approaches include **family attachment narrative therapy**. Parents face the challenge of sorting out their new roles and setting boundaries with regards to parenting, discipline, **financial obligations**, and time. Family therapy can help address these issues, and a therapy session also provides a platform for each member to voice his or her feelings in a respectful way. Children can express their **fears** and concerns and, through therapy, come to a better understanding about their place within the new family unit and may be reassured about their parent's continued love and affection for them. Parents might also learn ways to maintain a healthy relationship with their children while building a new and loving bond with their spouse and Blended children.

Tip # 79
Give it Time and Time it Right

Timing is usually everything when it comes to blending families. Keep in mind that jumping into a new marriage directly after a divorce or loss of a spouse may not be a good idea, for either parent or child. Sometimes the parent needs time to grow individually and focus on the child, while the child needs time to digest and adjust to the loss of one family before entering another. Blended families will also be more successful when there is a healthy parent-child relationship already established. Even if you give it lots of time, you still shouldn't assume that during the courting or after the wedding the family is going to become one big happy, cohesive unit. Having this expectation compromises everyone's ability to adjust at their own pace. Putting pressure on stepchildren to accept and love the new family can breed resentment.

Tip # 80

When should boys and girls stop using the same restroom?
Take time to create a space that is special for the children and gives them some personal ownership. There is an informal debate about whether opposite-sexed siblings should be allowed to share a bedroom and, if so, for how long. There are as many opinions on this topic as there are people giving them, so we decided to ask an expert to help clear up the confusion.
At what age do we suggest separating boys' and girls' bedrooms?
There isn't a specific age cutoff that requires that opposite-sex children separate rooms. Parents should monitor where their children are, developmentally, and make decisions from there.
Often, once children are in school, they begin to become aware of the need for modesty and may feel uncomfortable changing in front of an opposite-gender sibling; however, accommodations can be made for this, and children can change in other areas or at separate times. Yet, by the time children reach puberty, it will be much more difficult for them to feel comfortable sharing a room, and the need for privacy and space should be respected as much as possible.

Blended
Families
are
Awesome!

Tip # 81

What factors should parents look for when determining if they should separate the children?
If there is any concern that a child is acting out in a sexually aggressive way, it is important that the children be separated. If one or both children have ever been sexually abused, they may have difficulty understanding the clear boundaries associated with privacy. If a child expresses concern about privacy, families will benefit from taking those concerns seriously and work together to find an appropriate solution.

Tip # 82

What are the consequences if the children are not separated early enough?
Some families may see a lot of benefit from having children share bedroom space throughout their youth. The children may have a stronger bond with each other and feel comfortable sharing their things. Siblings may also find comfort in sleeping in the same room with a brother or sister. As children enter puberty, having space where they can feel comfortable with their bodies is important. Body image concerns may result in a child who feels uncomfortable or unsure of his or her body, [and] sharing a room may increase feelings of concern within a child

Tip # 83

How can parents deal with the situation if they just don't have enough room to separate them? (What are some alternatives?) Families who share rooms by necessity can find solutions for the problems. Children can be given their own specified space to keep clothes and toys in the bedroom. Providing an alternate space to change clothes, like the bathroom, or a schedule for the bedroom, can also help children learn the boundaries that are appropriate for privacy between genders.

Tip # 84

How should parents explain the separation to unwilling children who are used to being in the same room?
By emphasizing the benefits of having their own space, parents can encourage unwilling children to accept the change in sleeping arrangements. By taking time to create a space that is special for the children, parents can help children to feel excited about the change and give them some ownership over the new space.

Tip # 85

What if the boy and girl are Blended-siblings? Does that change things (for both Blended-siblings that are close in age and those that are far apart in age?)
This would mostly be a concern related to the age at which the children became Blended-siblings. If they were brought together at a young age … the situation would be very similar to biological siblings. Older children would benefit from having their own space.

Tip # 86

What if the step-siblings only see each other a few times each year? Does this change things?
Again, this would be relevant depending on the age of the Blended-siblings. Once a child reaches a point where he or she understands the need for modesty and privacy, it could be difficult to expect them to share space. However, if it were only a few times a year for short periods of time, it would most likely impact the children less than a

longer-term sharing of space.

Tip # 87

Focus on individual relationships
A Blended parent can set aside fifteen or thirty minutes (up to an hour each week) of special time with their Blended child. It's a time when the child gets to do whatever they want, within the limits of safety and reason. While avoiding instructing, teaching, or critiquing their Blended child, stepmom or stepdad is there to follow their stepchild's lead and to fill them with appreciation and respect. This is an opportunity to find common interests and create a space that feels safe and relaxed enough for both child and adult to really show one another who they are. These times can set the foundation for a strong and loving relationship between a Blended parent and Blended child.

Tip # 88

Couples need special time together as well. Stresses on all sides can mount quickly in Blended families, days can be busy, and alone time between couples can easily be put on the back burner. Make time at least once a month to be together without children— go to the movies, grab dinner, or squeeze in a walk during lunch time.

Tip # 89

Support children in their transitions
Moving back and forth from one household to another isn't easy. Transition days can be tough. It is a time when big feelings can erupt, and small incidents more easily set children off. If a child begins to cry about going to mommy's house, or about a granola bar she dropped as she was heading out the door, or a shirt she couldn't find, lean in, make eye contact, and listen. If a child is allowed to cry, instead of burying their feelings away, chances are their day will go better.

Making room for feelings to erupt as a child settles in after being away for a while or leaves for the other house can make a big difference. Be sure to build in extra time around transitions in case big feelings do surface so you can give your child extra attention in the hours before and after they change households.

Tip # 90

Use laughter to build closeness and reduce tension
Laughter and physical play can be the antidote to tension that arises in any family, and in blended families it can be used strategically during transition days or to build the relationship between Blended parents and Blended children, as well as between new and old siblings. In our household, we have a ritual of roughhousing after dinner. Wrestling and roughhousing are particularly helpful on the evenings that my Blended daughter returns to our house after being away for a few days.
Look for places where your children laugh and keep that laughter going. Be the goofy one who chases them through the house but can't quite catch them, let them be the victorious one, while you're the big, bumbling loser. Play and laughter can reduce tension and unify Blended families in a wonderful way.

Tip # 91

Find someone to listen to you

Whether it's the challenges of roughhousing, making the space for the storm of emotions that can erupt in any household, or the sadness of saying goodbye to a child as they go off with daddy, parents need someone they can talk to relieve the stress of parenting in a blended family. Talking about the stresses of blended families is an essential survival tool.

Find someone outside of your family to get support from. A friend, a neighbor, another parent or Blended parent—someone who can just listen without giving advice. Allow each person to take 15 to 30 minutes to talk, or cry, or laugh about how hard Blended families can be at times.

You can also use this time to talk about all the things that drive you crazy about your Blended child or biological child. Tell your listener the things you would never say to your children, and probably shouldn't say to your partner, but are important to get off your chest.

Tip # 92

Finding someone to talk to who won't jump in with their own experience or tell you how to handle your next conflict can be enormously refreshing and can eventually help you enjoy your Blended children (or your biological children) even more.

Find activities that unite, not alienate, Blended children and Blended parents. A Blended dad can feel like the odd parent out if mom and her daughter have a ritual of rollerblading every weekend and the Blended dad isn't so good on wheels. Find activities that Blended parents and Blended children can do together to bridge the gap. One Blended dad I know plays tennis with his Blended son every Saturday afternoon while the mom takes their daughters to swimming lessons.

Tip # 93

Always speak of other parents with respect

Although it may seem obvious, it's not always easy. In the heat of the moment when you're angry or frustrated at the parent who lives in the other household, keep negative comments or tension away from the children. All children want their parents to be respected (no matter how much conflict or hurt has ensued between them). And all parents deserve to be respected, even in their darkest moments. Children shouldn't be in the middle of or privy to conflict between parents who are separated.

What children really want is for their parents to get along. But because that's not always possible, at least be respectful of one another. Even if a parent is no longer in the picture and the child has lost all contact with their mother or father— we can still remind him that his mother who can no longer live with him will always love him.

Tip # 94

Find a respite from the storm

Even the most dedicated Blended parent can get exhausted, overwhelmed, and on the way to burn-out. Blended parents need a place to go to blow off steam and to feel connected with friends and other family. That might mean taking a good novel to another room of the house for a while or calling a loved one while walking around the block when things get to be too much. Or better yet, plan an overnight to a place in nature with a good friend. Just as parents need time to refuel and reconnect with people, they are close to, Blended parents also need a respite from the stress of Blended parenting.

Tip # 95

Merging two families

With more than half of all marriages ending in divorce, courting has become a whole new animal. Often, the people re-entering the courting pool after their marriages end are now adding children to their courting resumes. So, it's not surprising that when two people meet, fall in love and get married, they each have children.

Acknowledge the challenge.

All you want is for everyone in your new household to get along, right? But it's no small feat to combine two families into one as you co-parent with a new partner (along with your old one, whom you should never sabotage). Of course, it will take work to figure out how your new family unit will handle money, discipline, childcare and any other issues that you haven't mutually agreed upon yet. It can be an uphill climb at first, but it's doable once you have a plan.

Certain challenges, however, may be deal-breakers. If, for example, your new partner has made it clear that he is not willing to co-parent or to accept your children in your new home, that can't be OK with you. It's your job to stand up for your children, provide leadership, and work toward a solution.

Come up with a plan.
When a family merges, these are some of the topics that need to be discussed:
The role each parent will play in parenting and facilitating the development of any children.
The division of labor concerning the children.
Expectations in terms of how much space there will be for the couple to do things without children.
What kind of access grandparents and other extended family members will have.
Long-term goals and financial planning.

Tip # 96

Communicate before you cohabitate
No matter how great the relationships are between you and your new spouse and between the Blended siblings, once it's time to move in together, things can get (make that will get) tricky. Be prepared. Before you cohabitate, have family meetings. Children are smart and should be included in the decision making -- especially when it comes to things that are going to change their current set-up. If they feel like they are part of the process, they will be less anxious about the unknown.

Tip # 97
Consistency counts

Not only are families merging, but rules, discipline styles and communication tactics are also coming together. You and your spouse need to come to agreements on how to handle everything from bedtimes to homework to household chores. You are now **Blended parents** to each other's children for the first time, and it's important to have the same discipline approach to both your biological children and your Blended children. If there is a consistent message for the children coming from both of you on what's right and what's wrong, it will make the transition for the children (and you!) easier. As with anything, it will take time to find your stride.

Tip # 98

Check in so they don't check out

Silence doesn't mean acceptance. Everyone needs to feel heard, especially a child in a newly-blended family. Regular family meetings are a must. Use them as a time to talk about what's working and what's not. What's been frustrating and what's been fun? Ask everyone to come up with ideas for how to bond -- maybe you make a date with just his children and vice versa. Bottom line? Be sure you know how every child in the family is feeling.

Tip # 99

Be prepared to fail (and that's okay)

With so many personalities coming together, there's bound to be some bumps in the road. You and your spouse (and the children) will make mistakes. If you prepare yourself for the inevitable ups and downs that come along with blending families, you'll reduce stress, anxiety and disappointment. In the end, what matters most is that you're all together.

Tip # 100

Do start talking with your children about the possibility of blending your family, early. LONG before your marriage, begin the dialogue about the future family life. Mix in lots of listening so that all the children feel heard.

Tip # 101

Don't push your children into creating relationships. Allow those relationships to evolve slowly and naturally over time. Give your children the time, space and flexibility to adjust to the new situation.

Tip # 102

Do establish new traditions. Some current traditions and rituals you will want to maintain. Others you will need to create around the new family setting. Look for uniqueness in your new blended family and build a tradition around that.

Tip # 103

Don't expect your Blended children to call you Mom or Dad. Let the Blended children decide what they want to call you. Their comfort level is important here. If they don't naturally settle on a name, meet with them to mutually establish a name that you are comfortable being called.

Tip # 104
Do establish a unified parenting approach that is evenly applied to all in the family. Reach agreement with your new partner on how to address the important parenting situations that present themselves. Correct behavior from a position of, **"This is how we do it in our family."**

Tip # 105

Don't focus exclusively on the family and neglect strengthening your marriage. Raising children is a challenge. Raising other people's children is a special challenge. Having a strong marriage will help you manage the challenge of blending your families together.

Tip # 106
Do spend some time alone with each child and Blended children. Set aside time each day to connect one-on-one with all the children in your new family. This will help them establish a sense of belonging that enhances their connection to the family. Do hold family meetings. This gives all members of the family a chance to express their opinions and have input into the rules, schedule, and planning of upcoming events. Family meetings provide opportunities for family members to vent as well as express appreciation.

Tip # 106

Don't attempt to do it alone. Seek support from a local community organization or family therapist professional. Parents of blended families must sort out their new roles. They must set boundaries around parenting, discipline, and finances. Family therapy or counseling can help address these issues. **Therapy** can provide a platform for family members to voice their feelings.

Tip # 107
Try stepping in your children's shoes.
It's difficult to see things through someone else's eyes if you haven't walked in their shoes. Your children or Blended-children are passengers on this train; they didn't get the opportunity to choose whether they wanted a new family member, so great care and patience should be taken to help them adapt to the situation. Whether you're the Blended-parent or it's your spouse who's in that role, talk frequently with the children about how it's going and what the experience is from the other's point of view. If all of you have good intentions and a loving heart, you will work it out — but first you must communicate openly.

Tip # 108

Have discussions with your spouse outside of an argument.
If most of your discussions are taking place within the context of an argument, you need to stop. Agree to make time to talk calmly and rationally. This is important not only for you as you attempt to reach resolutions, but also for your children or Blended-children if they are within earshot. If they have already watched a divorce unfold, they have internalized plenty of parental conflict and may be shaken to their core. Don't make it worse. When you argue in front of children, you change who they are. For you, the fight is over when it's over. For your children, it doesn't end. They don't see you make up, and they don't participate in the healing. They go to bed at night thinking that their parents are fighting because of *them*.

Tip # 109

Stop complaining and be specific about your needs.
Tell your partner exactly what your needs are and what you need from them. Do you need to feel more special? Do you want your children to feel more accepted in their new home? Do you need a

different division of labor? Articulate your needs and explain precisely how they can be met. Nobody can read your mind. In turn, you need to ask your partner what is needed from you.

Tip # 110
Agree on discipline strategies for children.
Don't assume that your style of disciplining will be appropriate for your Blended children. It's important that you talk to your partner about the rules and punishment that existed before you joined the family. It's unfair to change the rules on a child overnight.

Tip # 111
Create a personal relationship with your Blended child(ren).
Make a commitment to developing a relationship with your Blended children that has nothing to do with your spouse. Set aside some special time in which you and the child can interact alone. You also need to stop thinking of your Blended child as **"his child"** or **"her child."** Make no doubt about it: You are now a pivotal person in that child's life too.
Tip # 112

Support your spouse's relationship with his/her child.
Don't make your spouse choose between you and their child. Your relationship with your spouse will not suffer if he / she has a close relationship with a child. We all have multiple **"accounts"** from which we draw our love. There's a child account that has an infinite amount of love in it, and there's a completely different account that you draw

from for your spouse. In other words, loving and nurturing your child in no way decreases the balance in the account for your spouse because they're two separate deals. With that in mind, ask your partner how you can help them nurture their relationship with a child; becoming their number one support system in building and maintaining it.

Tip # 113

Form an alliance with your former spouse.
You and your former spouse have not ended your relationship; instead, you have changed it from an intimate, emotional affiliation to a relationship that's held together by common goals for your children. Joining with your ex, unselfishly putting hurt feelings aside and leaving behind the pain of betrayal or a dysfunctional history are tremendous gifts to your children. To be cold, sabotaging, hurtful or exclusionary with your former spouse is, in some sense, to do the same for your children.

Tip # 114

Compartmentalize. When all members of a merging family are present, often feelings of **"being stuck in the middle"** or **"feeling left out"** surface from biological and Blended-parents. These emotional pulls are normal in merging families but can lead to overwhelming stress and anxiety. One way to reduce these emotional pulls and strengthen your merging family is to separate periodically and spend quality time with smaller units of the family. For example, a Blended parent may spend one on one time with their Blended child without the biological parent present.

Tip # 115

Keep negative comments about ex-spouses to yourself. Research continues to support that one of the primary sources of children's problems after a divorce is the inability of parents to keep negative feelings towards their ex (or their partner's ex) to themselves.

Tip # 116

Give children Time to Get to Know One Another First
Take it slow when trying to combine households. It is never a good idea to move in together until the children have gotten to know each other. This takes time and it is something to tread carefully and slowly with if you want to be successful at blending a family.

Tip # 117

Get on the Same Page with Your Partner
When parents remarry and bring children from their previous families together, each side brings its own discipline rules, traditions, and communication styles. That's why it's extra important for a newly married couple to get on the same page on everything from bedtimes to curfews. Both biological and step children need to receive consistent messages from both parents.
A house divided is a house that will not stand. The children must know that there is no division in the house and that no matter what, you and spouse are the adults.

Tip # 118

Keep Fights in Perspective
One of the perennial dilemmas of parenting is that children fight. Biological children, adopted children, Blended children, children down the street. Fighting is part of childhood. So, when two families try to merge, there will be battles, just as there are in any family situation. Be careful to keep the fights in perspective and pick your battles carefully.

Tip # 119

Hold Regular Family Meetings

In the process of blending 'yours, mine and ours,' it is especially important that everyone needs to feel heard, especially the children. One way to do so is hold regular family meetings, and to make time to listen to each child individually. Our best advice would be to have family meetings and talk out anything that is bothering them. You may have to deal with problems and headaches. The two oldest fight just like they are siblings, but when it comes down to it, they would be there for the other one. You must listen to their concerns and problems.

The best way to stay in touch with each child's feelings in blended families is to make time for each child individually. It is difficult with working full time and looking after the children and house, but you still must try and set aside time for your older children. Sometimes it's just talking about school, friends, or looking at stuff on the laptop with them. Older children may feel left out, and occasionally they will comment that they are looking after their little family members but by letting them stay up later occasionally or taking them out on a regular basis it improves dramatically.

Tip # 120

You will have a much more difficult time putting your marriage first.

Heidi Klum and Seal were often quoted saying their partnership came before parenting their four children, because it was best to have two solid, committed parents. With their divorce recently finalized, we all see how that worked out. If you are part of a blended family, chances are you've already spent time as a single parent where your children came first. Switching up the order is tough and causes hurt feelings. Don't get us wrong—the order is going to switch practically every minute and if one of those minutes collides with your partner in the same spot, literally and physically, well than that's just magic.

Tip # 121
You are more set in your ways than you realize.

All it takes is a child or two (or three) and a spouse to show you just how much you prefer your way, because chances are that you have been the head-of-household adult making the decisions for a while.

Tip # 122

You will have a hard time not comparing this life to the life you had before.

Because this life was chosen so carefully. Because, no matter how you went into your past marriage, this marriage you went into with your eyes wide open. But...having a comparison will often prove to you what a smart choice you made.

Tip # 123
You might be jealous of the ex.

Even if they are the craziest man or woman on the planet, and the thought that he / she would have chosen you in the same lifetime makes you question everything that got you here in the first place. The fact that their DNA has blended and formed little humans is a connection that surpasses every level of certifiable crazy.

Tip # 124

You will love your new spouses' children.
You will even love them well. Maybe right away, maybe it will take years. But you will. You will hold them to the same expectations as you hold your own children. Your heart will break and soar when theirs does. Their accomplishments will provide pride, their setbacks will break your heart. They will be the closest thing ever to your own children. Maybe you will experience a love extremely close to that of the love for your own children. Or maybe it will always be just a bit shy. Either way, you will love them as you need to, as they need it.

Tip # 125

You will never be comfortable with even the slightest negative comment about your children, even if it comes from the spouse you have promised to love no matter what.
It may as well be written in the vows, **"through sickness and health, til death or you saying something mean about my children, do we part."** You can complain about your children being bratty or needy or driving you crazy, but your spouse, the Love of Your Life, must find them to be wonderful every moment and if they don't, they should keep it to themselves forever and ever.

Tip # 126

You forgive easier.
Because you must. There is a whole slew of people requiring your forgiveness daily. People who haven't known you long and want to take your patience out for a test drive. And there will be a lot more things that require forgiveness. Balance in a Blended Family Requires Forgiveness! Remarried couples, with children to raise, are often blindsided by a swarm of unexpected problems that feel a whole lot like stepping into a hornets' nest unaware. There is no other family

dynamic where forgiveness given contributes such a big plus. Absorbing the impact of two or three outside homes, fated to affect life under our roof, isn't easy to put up with and it is a unique dynamic that no biological family ever experiences. With a great measure of tact, we are cornered into considering all the people involved—like it or not. Disagreements always center on either children or money.

Tip # 127

You will become more private about things.
If only because it means not having to explain to a stranger at Target how five children shot out of your uterus like rapid fire. Or because you get sick of people asking, **"Which ones are yours?"**
In blended families, trouble with territory can frequently cause simmering tension and full-scale battles. When children who previously had their own rooms are forced to share, this can be especially problematic. If there isn't enough space for each child to have their own room, ensure there is an allocated area of the room just for them. Create dividers in a shared bedroom with curtains or inventive re-arrangements of the furniture. Also provide them with somewhere to put their special belongings – a box or drawer that is respected by other family members as a private no-go zone.

Tip # 128

You will have no road map.
While there are a thousand books about blended families, none of them will be able to speak to your exact situation. Helpful advice will often be only the bits and pieces you can relate to that you have to fuse together yourself. Sometimes you will find yourself as a **partner supporting an ex-spouse.** One partner or both partners may have financial obligations to their former spouse in terms of a divorce order, and this should be discussed openly and accounted for in the monthly budget.
Financial obligations in terms of a divorce order can be amended only

in terms of an order of court. There may be many reasons the former wife did not work, including the possibility that her ex-husband wanted her to stay at home to look after their daughter. These two families approached the matter maturely and were able to resolve their problems. However, this is not the norm, and these all-important issues should be addressed before making a long-term commitment to someone who has financial obligations to his (or her) previous spouse.

Sometimes you may be **a widow and a widower, each with children** When a family experiences the loss of a beloved spouse and parent, the new Spouse/ Blended parent will inevitably confront the **"ghosts of family past."** On some level, grieving continues for years after the death of a spouse.

This Blended family needs to make sure it is taking steps to heal from their grief for the new family to unite. Rather than trying to assume a parental role, the successful Blended parent in this situation will Blended into the role of friend and mentor. Family members can honor their loved one with photographs and memories but erecting a shrine and idolizing their past prevents intimacy with the new spouse and Blended parent. Establishing common ground and moving forward together is difficult but possible.

A husband must make provision for his family financially. It is wonderful that each partner is financially stable and can support his or her own children. This is the ideal situation, because it removes financial stress from the newly formed family. Again, this is not the norm, and a surviving spouse is often left inadequately provided for. We recently had a client whose ex-husband passed away at the age of 51. He died quite convinced that he had provided more than enough for his children. However, he had received incorrect estate planning advice, and the impact of capital gains tax, estate duty and other taxes had not been factored into the calculations. Although he had assured his children that they would have "millions" when he died, the reality was quite different.

Sometimes you will have Children from a previous marriage and your own baby

In a blended family, there may be an imbalance in, for example, the financial resources allocated to each child, or how much has been saved for the education of each child.

It can be difficult to ensure that your children receive "the same" as your Blended-children. Instead of trying to make sure that the same amount is spent on each child – which is almost impossible given their different needs – the emphasis should be on what is fair. The children need to understand that they have different needs at different stages of their life, and everyone's needs will be treated fairly.

Tip # 129

A financial roadmap is crucial for the future stability of a newly formed family, and an independent financial adviser can be instrumental in mapping out a plan. Second marriages can bring a special set of financial challenges, and one of those is figuring out what money rules will govern the new blended family.

If the merging families came from different income brackets, they may be used to handling money in different ways, including what kinds of things the parents buy for their children.

But even in couples from similar financial backgrounds, the two parents may have different philosophies on chores, allowances and savings strategy. The rules that were negotiated with the previous spouse may not sit well with the new spouse. And as a single parent, you might have gotten used to making all your own rules, without consulting anyone else, when it comes to family finances.

There's a new you now. You've got two people coming together to create a new family and a new dynamic.

Honest and open communication about each spouse's financial affairs is the starting point of this journey.

Tip # 130

It's hard enough for a child to compete with siblings in a nuclear family. When it's Blended-siblings that they're not entirely comfortable with, the problem can magnify. For a child who hasn't had to share a parent in a long time, that adjustment period might be a little bit longer.

First, talk to your spouse so you're on the same page about sibling rivalry. Nothing will work if one of you blames the other person's biological child for causing the rift. If you have different disciplinary styles, you're also likely to encounter problems.

Consequences and rewards need to be the same for all the children, no matter how it **"used to work"** before you two got married.

Next, remember that in some way, your children may be more like strangers than siblings. So, don't expect everyone to be "one big happy family" in the beginning. It will take a while to get to that point. If there was a change-up in birth order—that is, one child who was previously the oldest is now stuck in the middle—acknowledge the resentment that could cause. The previously eldest child probably felt like she had a little bit of power that's now been taken away from her, while the former baby of the house might feel like he's lost the attention he once had.

Avoid placing labels on your children as well. Even positive labels like, "She's the musician in our family," and "He's our star athlete," can increase tension among family members. Point out that everyone has many skills and talents and it's healthy to keep exploring new areas of interest.

Tip # 131

Everyone Needs Attention

When the number of children increases, as it frequently does in blended families, one or all the children might feel like they're not getting the attention that they're used to.

Additionally, blended families sometimes have less time and money for each child's extracurricular activities or for family outings because of the increase in family size.

As with so many other issues, this problem can be resolved—to the best of its ability, anyway—by working together as a family. Create a set schedule that everyone has weighed in on, with each child choosing an activity within a certain budget throughout the month. Additionally, both adults should attend each child's activities, such as sporting games, plays or concerts, so it doesn't feel like any child is being favored over another.

Give each child individual attention as well. Whether you play a quick game together for 10 minutes every day or you schedule a once-a-month outing, giving biological children and stepchildren plenty of positive attention can strengthen your bond.

Tip # 132

You Feel Like Two Separate Families

You and your new spouse want to feel like one unit that can have fun, share, and rely on each other. The children aren't entirely comfortable with each other, though, nor with their new Blended parent. It feels like you're still acting as two families that just happen to live in the same house.

You can't forge a bond overnight. It will take to time gain shared history, figure out new relationships and adapt to the new normal. Start the process slowly by beginning new traditions as a family. They might be reading a book together every night in the big bed in the master bedroom or taking a trip to the local playground every Sunday morning before breakfast.

You can also smooth the transition of going from house to house, a process that might happen regularly if you or your spouse have joint custody.

It's also important to give children time to grieve. While a new marriage can be happy, it also signals the end of the previous family dynamics. And that can be tough for children who are still struggling to deal with the fact that their biological parents are no longer together or that their time of being an only child with heaps of attention has come to an end.

Despite problems, a blended family is still just that—a family. Although there might be growing pains, squabbles and a few moments of discipline, everyone will eventually adjust to the new situation. Mistakes will be made, by children and by adults, but everyone will learn from those mistakes. Eventually, the household will feel less like a mish-mash of families and more like one solid unit.

Tip # 133

If you're like most parents, you may struggle to list your household rules off the top off your head. Although you know what behaviour is acceptable (and what isn't), labelling your expectations may be a little tricky.

That's why it's important to create a written list of household rules. Then, everyone in the family becomes clear about your expectations. Rules also help children feel safe and secure. When your rules are clear, you'll be less likely to get into power struggles. Your child's attempts to say, **"But Mom, I didn't know!"** won't be effective when you remind him of the list of rules.

What to Include

Household rules should include the rules that EVERYONE in the house is expected to follow, including parents. So, don't include, **"Bedtime is at 7 p.m.,"** unless you also plan to go to bed at that time.

Your household rules should be specific to your family's needs and values. While it might be important to one family to say, **"No jumping on the furniture,"** another family may want a rule that says, **"Try at least two bites of everything on your plate."**

A lengthy list of rules could become too complicated and confusing, so keep your list short and simple. Here is a sample list of household

rules:
Treat Other People and Their Property With Respect
These rules may include:

- Do not hurt anyone's feelings (no yelling, put-downs, or name-calling).

- Do not hurt anyone's body (no hitting, pushing, or kicking).

- Ask permission to borrow other people's belongings.

Implement an immediate consequence if this rule gets broken. Time-out, loss of privileges or other forms of discipline can help children learn to make better choices. This is a good rule for parents as well as children as you need to model appropriate behaviour and anger control.

Tip # 134

Knock on Closed Doors Before Entering
Teach children about privacy by establishing a rule about knocking on closed doors before entering. This can help reinforce the idea that you should respect other people's space.

Tip # 135

Pick Up After Yourself
Explain what it means to pick up after yourself. Tell your child to put her dishes in the dishwasher when she's done eating. Or explain that you expect your children to pick up their toys before they get out new toys. This rule enhances household safety and cleanliness and develops good habits for when your children will go on to live independently.
Electronics Curfew
Many families establish rules about electronics. While some families

limit screen time to a couple of hours per day, others set rules about what time electronics need to be turned off. Setting a curfew for electronics before bedtime can help develop good sleep hygiene for both children and parents which enables you to get a better night's sleep for health.

Make Amends When You Hurt Someone

Teach children to take responsibility for their behaviour by creating a rule about how to respond if they've hurt someone. Sometimes an apology may be enough and at other times, you may need to institute restitution consequently.

Tip # 136

Tell the Truth

Stressing the importance of honesty will only be effective if you role model the behaviour you want to see from your children. If you tell your children to always tell the truth, but claim your 13-year-old is only 12 so you can get a lower-priced movie ticket, your words won't be effective. Children can't tell the difference between **"big white lies"** and other lies so if you're going to stress the importance of honesty, show that you're honest.

Tip # 137

Complete Your Dental and Body Hygiene Routines

Washing hands, brushing teeth, and bathing must be done for good health. Establish these as a rule so your children develop good habits, and don't shirk them yourself.

Tip # 138

Attend Family Meetings Once a Week

Holding regularly scheduled family meetings can help you review the rules, talk about schedules, and make any changes as necessary. While some families may want to schedule a meeting once a week, other families may find that meeting once a month is plenty.

Tip # 139

Revise Your List as Needed

Work together as a family to problem-solve specific issues. For example, if you're noticing that several family members aren't picking up after themselves, talk about it and see what you can do to better enforce this rule.

Be open to revising the list of rules as needed. As your children grow and mature, the behaviours you'll want to address will shift as well. Add new rules when necessary.

Tip # 140

To err is human and making discipline mistakes is a part of being a parent. Your child misbehaves, and you find yourself losing your cool, yelling, or reacting in a way that you think could have been handled better. There are ways to fix these common blunders. Visualize yourself reacting differently to your child the next time he does something to make you crazy and be confident in your ability to change his / her bad behaviour—and your reaction to his behaviour. Remember to give yourself a break. These discipline mistakes are common because most parents make one or more of these at one time or another.

Common Mistakes Parents Make When Disciplining Children

Remind yourself of the advice you might give your child when he makes an error. Mistakes are what you learn from so that you can grow.

You Weren't Respectful to Your Child

Parents ask their children to respect them, but they sometimes forget that respect should be a two-way street. One of the most common mistakes parents make when disciplining children is yelling, speaking in a harsh and angry tone, or even insulting their children. Giving and asking for respect in return is one of the cardinal tips to remember about disciplining children.

Tip # 141

Think about how you would like to be spoken to if you were working out a conflict with an adult, such as a co-worker or relative. Get down to your child's eye level and discuss the problem at hand in a gentle (but still firm) and respectful manner. No matter how angry you are, try to remain calm. Do not yell, and never belittle your child.

Tip # 142

Disciplining While Angry

There are some things that just should not go together, like drinking and driving or writing a heated email to someone who's made you angry before you've had a chance to cool down. Disciplining a child while angry is in that category of don'ts. When you reprimand your child while you're mad about something they did, you are more likely to shout or say something you don't mean.

Take a few minutes (or more if you need it) to calm down and collect your thoughts before talking to your child about his bad behaviour. Remove yourself or your child from the immediate situation. Take a walk. Giving yourself and your child some time to reflect on the conflict may help you both deal with the situation in a calmer manner.

Tip # 143

Being Inconsistent

You reprimand your child for not cleaning his room but ignore it when his room is messy for days. Then once again you scold him for not keeping his room clean. Your child is getting a very inconsistent message. One of the best ways to help children correct their behaviour is by giving them clear instructions about what is expected of them.

Give your child clear and simple directions and a realistic list of expectations. For instance, if you want him to clean his room every week, mark it on a calendar and make that "room clean-up day." Set him up for good behaviour. If he does not follow through, give him a consistent set of consequences. Don't give different degrees of punishments for the same misbehaviour. Be constant and consistent in enforcing the rules.

Tip # 144

Talking or Explaining Too Much

Giving a lengthy and detailed explanation of your child's inappropriate behaviour is not a good idea. Children, even grade-schoolers who are getting better at paying attention, can easily lose track of discussions that go too much into detail.

Be as direct as possible and break it down into basics for your child. With older children, talk about what went wrong and discuss possible scenarios that could have been better choices. With younger children, simply state what the behaviour was and why it was wrong (**"You went into your brother's room and played with his toy without his permission, and that made him feel like you didn't care about his feelings."**)

Tip # 145

Going Negative

Hearing a string of **"don't"** and **"no"** isn't any fun for anyone, especially a child. Focusing on what a child did wrong or what he should not do instead of emphasizing what a child should do can put a negative spin on things and set the tone for your interaction. Approach things from a more positive perspective by talking about what can be done better. If your child is whining or talking back to you, show her some examples of how to speak in a nice and more friendly manner. After tempers have cooled on both sides, try a light-hearted game of speaking nicely to each other to express yourselves better. If your child is fighting with a sibling, suggest some ways they can build a good sibling relationship, such as by having them work together on a project.

Tip # 146

Thinking That Disciplining Means Punishing

Often, parents forget that the point of disciplining children is to give them firm guidelines and limits so that they do not need to be punished. Disciplining means setting up boundaries and expectations so that children know what is expected of them. The primary goal is to have children learn to eventually regulate themselves so that they do not need to be punished.

Re-think the way you view discipline. When you discipline a child, you are showing him / her how to make good choices and choose behaviours that are positive and ultimately good for her. And by showing her how you handle her misbehaviour—in a loving and constructive manner that emphasizes learning rather than punishment—you are teaching him / her how to one day interact with their own children when they demonstrate bad behaviour.

Tip # 147

Not Practicing What You Preach
You tell your child not to tell lies but routinely fib to get out of things you don't want to do like join that school volunteer committee or attend an unimportant meeting at work. You yell at your children and angrily tell them to speak nicely to each other. The problem is that you often do not see your own behaviour and forget that your children are watching your every move and learning how to behave by using your example.

As much as possible, be a good example of the behaviour you want your child to emulate. If you occasionally break one of your own rules, explain to your child the circumstances and why you behaved the way you did. Explore how you could have handled it better and talk about how you may do things differently the next time.

Tip # 148

Not Fitting the Discipline Technique to Your Child
When it comes to child discipline, one size does not fit all. What worked on a child's sibling or the children of friends may be the wrong approach for a child. Repeatedly trying to use a certain approach to correct or guide a child's behaviour might not work best for an individual child.

Remember that children, like adults, have their own personalities, temperaments, and quirks. One child may be more stubborn than others or be more likely to have a meltdown when things don't go his way. Try different approaches to tailor discipline techniques to each individual child.

For instance, while one child may be able to focus and stop dawdling after a few general reminders, another child may need charts, schedules, and closer supervision to keep him on track. One child may stop misbehaving after a warning that he will lose privileges (a toy or an activity), while another child may need to have those things taken away and experience the consequences of bad behaviour before he learns to follow the rules.

Tip # 149

Not Disciplining Children at All
Among the many important reasons why you need to discipline children is the fact that children who are raised with clear limits and guidance are more likely to be happy, pleasant people who have good self-control. When children are not disciplined, the effects are clear, and in most cases, quite catastrophic. Children who are not given any limits or consequences and are spoiled are often selfish, unable to self-regulate, and unpleasant to be around.
Give your child rules, limits, and clear and consistent consequences when they don't do what they are supposed to do. If you are worried that disciplining your child may make him angry with you, keep the bigger picture in mind. Not disciplining a child is not good for him. If you handle his misbehaviour with love and firm guidance, your child will learn and grow from his mistakes.

Tip # 150

Financial and living arrangements.
Adults should agree on where they will live and how they will share their money. Most often partners embarking on a second marriage report that moving into a new home, rather than one of the partner's prior residences, is advantageous because the new environment becomes **"their home."** Couples also should decide whether they want to keep their money separate or share it. Couples who have used the **"one-pot"** method generally reported higher family satisfaction than those who kept their money separate.

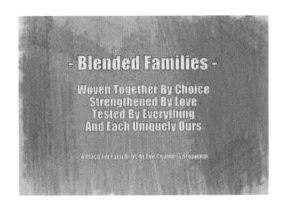

Tip # 151

Resolving feelings and concerns about the previous marriage.
Remarriage may resurrect old, unresolved anger and hurts from the previous marriage, for adults and children. For example, hearing that her parent is getting remarried, a child is forced to give up hope that the custodial parents will reconcile. Or a woman may exacerbate a stormy relationship with her ex-husband, after learning of his plans to remarry, because she feels hurt or angry.
Anticipating parenting changes and decisions. Couples should discuss the role the Blended parent will play in raising their new spouse's children, as well as changes in household rules that may have to be made. Even if the couple lived together before marriage, the children are likely to respond to the Blended parent differently after remarriage because the Blended parent has now assumed an official parental role.

Tip # 152

Marriage quality
While newlywed couples without children usually use the first months of marriage to build on their relationship, couples with children are often more consumed with the demands of their children. Young children, for example, may feel a sense of abandonment or competition as their parent devotes more time and energy to the new spouse. Adolescents are at a developmental stage where they are more sensitive to expressions of affection and sexuality and may be

---

disturbed by an active romance in their family.

Couples should make priority time for each other, by either making regular dates or taking trips without the children.

Tip # 153
Parenting in Blended families

The most difficult aspect of Blended family life is parenting. Forming a Blended family with young children may be easier than forming one with adolescent children due to the differing developmental stages. Adolescents, however, would rather separate from the family as they form their own identities.

Recent research suggests that younger adolescents (age 10-14) may have the most difficult time adjusting to a Blended family. Older adolescents (age 15 and older) need less parenting and may have less investment in Blended family life, while younger children (under age 10) are usually more accepting of a new adult in the family, particularly when the adult is a positive influence. Young adolescents, who are forming their own identities tend to be a bit more difficult to deal with.

Blended parents should at first establish a relationship with the children that is more akin to a friend or **"camp counselor,"** rather than a disciplinarian. Couples can also agree that the custodial parent remain primarily responsible for control and discipline of the children until the Blended parent and children develop a solid bond.

Until Blended parents can take on more parenting responsibilities, they can simply monitor the children's behavior and activities and keep their spouses informed.

Families might want to develop a list of household rules. These may include, for example, "We agree to respect each family member," or **"Every family member agrees to clean up after him or herself."**

Tip # 154

Blended parent - child relations

While new Blended parents may want to jump right in and to establish a close relationship with Blended children, they should consider the child's emotional status and gender first.
Both boys and girls in Blended families have reported that they prefer verbal affection, such as praises or compliments, rather than physical closeness, such as hugs and kisses. Girls especially say they're uncomfortable with physical shows of affection from their Blended father. Overall, boys appear to accept a Blended father more quickly than girls.

Tip # 155

Nonresidential parent issues
After a divorce, children usually adjust better to their new lives when the parent who has moved out visits consistently and has maintained a good relationship with them.
But once parents remarry, they often decrease or maintain low levels of contact with their children. Fathers appear to be the worst perpetrators: On average, dads drop their visits to their children by half within the first year of remarriage.
The less a parent visits, the more a child is likely to feel abandoned. Parents should reconnect by developing special activities that involve only the children and parent.
Parents shouldn't speak against their ex-spouses in front of the child because it undermines the child's self-esteem and may even put the child in a position of defending a parent.

Tip # 156

Marriages with blended families tend to be very unsuccessful, one of the greatest predictors of divorce. It is common for each spouse to put his or her own children's interests first. It is often to compensate for the trauma children experience when there is a divorce. But when the children's interests are first, the interests of the other spouse and the other spouse's children are found somewhere down the list, and that's a formula for marital disaster.

Never do anything without an enthusiastic agreement between you and your spouse. In effect, whenever you follow this policy, you put your spouse's interests first, where they should be.

Following this policy means that neither you nor your spouse act to reprimand or discipline any child until you have reached an enthusiastic agreement about it. At first, you may not agree about much of anything, in which case you are not to discipline the children (they may do whatever they please). But as you practice applying the policy, you and your spouse will begin to establish guidelines in child-rearing issues, and agreements will start to form. Eventually, you will agree on how to discipline your children in a way that takes each other's feelings into account, and your marriage will be saved.

Tip # 157

Child rearing is a huge problem in blended families, but it's not the only issue in your marriage. Regardless of your conflicts, however, you'll find that you can resolve them all when you have learned to negotiate and agree with each other.

Here are a few guidelines that will help you negotiate an enthusiastic agreement:

Set ground rules to make negotiations pleasant and safe:

a) try to be pleasant and cheerful through your discussion of the issue,

b) put safety first--do not threaten to cause pain or suffering when you negotiate, even if your spouse makes threatening remarks or if the negotiations fail,

c) if you reach an impasse, stop for a while and come back to the issue later.

Identify the problem from the perspectives of both you and your husband. Be able to state the other spouse's position before you go on to find a solution.

Brainstorm solutions with abandon. Spend some time thinking of all sorts of ways to handle the problem, and don't correct each other when you hear of a plan that you don't like. You'll have a chance to do that later.

Choose the solution that is appealing to both of you. And if your brainstorming has not given you an answer that you can enthusiastically agree upon, go back to brainstorming.

The reason you argue is that you are incompatible -- you have not learned how to act in the interest of both of you at the same time. Learn to negotiate and agree with each other. Eventually, your marriage will turn out better than you could have ever hoped.

If you don't follow this policy, however, you will eventually make each other so miserable that you will lose your love for each other and divorce, like most marriages with blended families. This process has already begun. Stop it before it goes any further.

Tip # 158

Common sense is one of our best allies in relationships. Treat each other with kindness, patience and respect -- the way you like to be treated. Refrain from speaking ill of their other natural parent at all cost. When two separate families come together under one roof, there are going to be conflicts. However, talking about them and understanding the other's feelings is necessary and critical. It will take time to build a history with each other that will someday grow from affection into familial love. It may take time and probably won't be easy, but it is well worth the effort.

Tip # 159

Blended Families – Parents and Children

The first and foremost rule for blended families is that parents DO NOT disagree with each other in front of the children. When spouses have a conflict -- any conflict -- it should be discussed behind closed doors. It is very tempting to stand up for your own child and point a finger at the Blended child. It is equally tempting to accuse your spouse of unbalanced discipline toward your child. Do not allow yourself to be guilty of the same. "Remember, the children are thrown together with near strangers and suddenly feel they have to vie for their parent's attention. They often feel they are being replaced rather than added to. It is so important for children to see a united front and stable relationships for a change. The most common problem is discipline which can quickly disrupt this unity. You must work with your spouse to unite your discipline ideas and styles. Early on, the natural parent needs to talk to their children and reaffirm the control and respect due the Blended parent. Back up your spouse! Whether children lost a parent due to death or divorce, their lives have changed. When the children knew ahead of time what was expected of them their acceptance of the new family became easier.

Tip # 160

New personalities, customs, and memories are all added to the new household of blended families. However, it is still basic that a child is the child and an adult is still the adult. Children need a balance of love and discipline. Give your Blended children their 'much needed' affection, as you do your own children. (The loving feelings will grow in time as you do this.) It is the role of every parent to obey their responsibility of properly raising children. And children have a responsibility to honor their parents. Children do not have the maturity to understand the dynamics of this new family and how loving it could be; but as adults we should. Much like when couples adopt a child, we chose to marry into a family with these children. Care for them, nurture them, and accept them even when they seem to push away. We pray a lot for them and with them.

Tip # 161

Identity Confusion
Several aspects of forming a new family can create identity issues for young children. If the mother's name changes to the last name of the new husband while the children of the mother keep their own last name, children may feel suddenly abandoned.
Another common identity issue is for children to feel confused about their feelings for a blended-parent. While many children dislike the new spouse or partner at the start, positive feelings often develop quickly. While this may seem like a positive thing, it can cause difficulties for children sorting out their feelings for their real father versus the father they live with on a day-to-day basis.

Tip # 162

Legal Disputes
Two families becoming one can add to the legal issues that arose when each original family separated. In a divorce, one partner may get the family house, but when a new partner comes into the picture, the legal agreements may need to be changed. Financial difficulties can arise from ongoing legal disputes or mediation fees.

Tip # 163

Financial Difficulties

Blended families often have large numbers of children, and all the costs associated with raising them. Money may be scarce because of divorce proceedings. Solving these financial issues is difficult but can take a large amount of worry off the shoulders of the parents. Get help from a financial advisor to get your finances on track; consult a lawyer if you think you are not receiving enough child support or are paying too much in alimony to your ex. Blending finances in blended families is difficult, but with a little help you can get things in order.

Tip # 164

Infringing on Territory

Children in blended families often have difficulties with one another's turf. If one half of the new family moves into the home of the other half, expect considerable amounts of fights and tears in the first few months. The children whose home it originally was may feel threatened by others taking over parts of their space; the children moving into the home will not be happy either because they feel like the place is not 'theirs' and they are not welcome.

If you can't, as a family, move into a new home together, try the following tips to reduce territorial issues:

Start from square one on bedrooms: everybody swaps, even the parents

If there are not enough bedrooms, make the den into one, or finish the basement

If children must share rooms, make sure the children have an active voice in dividing the room and decorating it

Clear out all drawers and closets in family spaces (marker drawers, closets full of games, etc.) and start from scratch putting away all family members' belongings

Keep each family member's allotted space as equal as possible

Remember that territory will include items as well as space. Create schedules for who may use the family computer when, and how long each child may play the PlayStation. Encourage the children to share and provide praise or rewards when they do so.

Tip # 165

Scheduling Conflicts
Coordinating after-school schedules can be difficult. As with organizing the house, try to give each child equal amounts of time and extra-curricular opportunities.

Scheduling in time with the parent with whom each child is no longer living can also throw a wrench in the scheduling. A few different options exist:

Have all the children go to their other parent on the same weekend each month to ensure the children are all in the blended family enough to bond with one another and work out the issues that arise.

Have all the children go to their other parent on alternate weekends so that you have time to share with your own children without the new siblings being present.

On a week-to-week rotation schedule, ensure that the children are not ships passing in the night. If your children are in your house on week one, and then leave in week two, when your partner's children are with you, becoming a family will present even more challenges. It's essential that the children live together under one roof in order to form a blended family, but it's also nice to have their biological parents to themselves sometimes.

Tip # 166

Utilize the Grandparents
Grandparents may worry they will lose contact with their grandchildren or their adult son or daughter. Relationships with the parents of the grandchildren come into play. Also, **geographical distance can be hard to overcome**. It's important to not distinguish between biological and non-biological grandchildren except as their interests and personalities differ. Sometimes the grandparents will be closer to some than to others, but that will have more to do with proximity and personality (as well as parental influence) than anything else.

Some say that feeling differently about biological grandchildren and step-grandchildren can be explained by what is sometimes called kin altruism or kin selection. That term simply means that as biological creatures we are disposed to favor those who share our genes, in order that our genes be perpetuated in the future. This explanation strikes some as logical, while others prefer to believe that humans should be able to overcome any biological biases that exist.

At any rate, humans may not be in total control of their hearts, but they can strive to control their behavior. And gift-giving is one practice that can be problematical.

On gift-giving occasions, there's seldom any excuse for unequal treatment, because a missing gift or a gift that is clearly inferior is an overt form of discrimination. But, again, grandparents often give more generous gifts to some grandchildren than to others, even when all the children are biological. Gifts for older children tend to be more expensive than those for younger children, just to mention one factor.

Also, if one set of grandchildren is needier than another set, the grandparents may give more to the ones who need it the most.

So how is a grandparent to ensure that a blended-grandchild doesn't feel slighted? One way is to think which biological grandchild the blended-grandchild is the most likely to compare gifts with and ensure that they have equal gifts. A first-grader probably will not know or care if you spend more on a college-age grandchild, but if her cousin of the same age gets more or better gifts, it will be noticed.

Tip # 167
When children come to visit

Many children spend time at two homes. This can be hard for everyone to get used to. Parents may:

feel overwhelmed by the extra children in the house

be upset about the amount of time their partner spends with their children.

Children who are visiting may:

feel jealous of other children living in the home full-time

feel like a burden, or that they are not wanted.

Children living in the home full-time may resent the visiting children. They may have to share their bedroom, or think the other child gets special attention.

When children come to visit:

give them time to adjust when they arrive. They may want to be alone for a while before joining in

let them know they are loved and that they have a place in your life

try to give them privacy, and a space of their own

help them sort out the things they want to leave at your house or bring each time. Don't be upset if they forget something.

Try to be consistent with family rules for all children.

Teenagers

Adolescence is a time of growing independence from parents. Young people are going through rapid physical and brain changes that can make them more emotional, irrational and likely to take risks. This is all normal and it is often a difficult time for families. Settling into a blended family can be an added pressure.

Some young people may be happy about the new arrangements, while others may not. It may depend on their previous history and relationships, their age and temperament, and what else is going on in their lives.

Young people may:

want to spend more time with friends than family

resent the new partner or their children, and not really want to be involved

be dealing with other issues in their lives.

It can help to:

understand what's going on for your young person and be patient with them. Don't take any outbursts or negative behavior personally

give them a say in things that affect them, such as who they live with

don't make big issues of small things – save it for what's important, such as safety

talk when things are calm – shouting matches don't help anyone

respect their privacy, and ensure others do too – give them space and time to adjust expect them to be involved in family chores and activities. If they resist, it can help to say you understand how they feel. Let them know you value their involvement and it is important for them to be part of the family. Come to agreements together rather than getting into a battle.

You don't have to be best friends with your teenager. Let them know you expect to be treated with respect – as you treat them with respect. Violence is never acceptable.

Looking after your relationship

The relationship with your partner is what holds the new family together. It is important to keep it strong, so you can work as a team and deal with the ups and downs. Try to spend quality time together without children.

Tip # 168

It's a second chance at success

It wasn't long ago that unhappy couples felt obliged to stay together: Divorce was a taboo that brought with it a social stigma. Today, it appears that Blended families can offer new nourishing relationships after the initial adjustment period. More than 60 percent of married adults with step-relatives say their marriage is closer than their parents' marriage, but only 45 percent of married adults without them say the same thing.

Tip # 169

Be sure He / She is worthy of an introduction

Thanks to online dating and social media, your single life can move at the speed of WiFi. (You can now download an application on Facebook that alerts you when friends change their status to "single".) While there may be no shortage of suitors, be careful whenever you introduce a **"special friend"** to your children. Some children get attached to people quickly, so it's hard on them when they suddenly aren't around anymore. Make sure the one you bring home is important to you.

Tip # 170

Add the ingredients and mix slowly

Group outings can be draining in the beginning (everyone's trying to get to know each other and be on their best behavior). Moving in a big pack during activities can set children up for competition—they'll often spend the time trying to attract Mom's or Dad's attention and steer it away from the new spouse. The fix? Focus first on having the steps get to know each other, one on one, rather than trying to mix it up too much.

Tip # 171

Discipline is a joint effort, but each of you has a different role

When it comes to dealing with less-than-stellar behavior, it's the parent who has the final say. Kevin's stricter about enforcing the rules, and I'm pretty much the **'fun one.'"** Blended parents shouldn't put up with a bunch of sass, but for children who are still adjusting to the new setup, being polite can be a lot to ask. If they're acting up, a Blended parent is better off relaying the information to the Biological parent, especially early on, rather than acting.

Tip # 172

A little patience makes a big difference

A strong bond from the original family can serve to squeeze out newcomers at first. A toddler or preschooler may cling desperately to Mom, refusing to separate at the appointed drop-off time; older children may pull away both physically and emotionally, and may even feel guilty about loving a blended family. Patience is key, as children of all ages will need lots of time to adjust to the new family dynamic. During this adjustment period, the onus is on the adults to show a vested interest in their new Blended children. Sit down and build blocks or play catch with little ones; attend an older child's swim meet or teach her to make food you both like. Be supportive by showing an interest in her activities and friends. Little by little, they'll start to let you into their life.

Tip # 173

When you don't want children of your own
This is one of the things you need to talk about before you agree to marry. There are so many arguments that you will avoid by just talking with one another about this future marriage. Many of us are so afraid to talk about real things and or we don't be the one to bring it up. You must bring up uncomfortable things in relationships. You must force a discussion on an important matter such as this. If you cannot have children for this man, then you must tell him. If you don't want her getting pregnant how will you prevent it. Women have much to lose in this area, so you must speak up. All courtship does not lead to marriage nor should it.

Tip # 174

Maintain traditions from your original family

Acknowledge that you are two families with your two histories coming together.
Discuss some old traditions that you want to continue doing.
Determine if you want to make new traditions.
Anything is fair game as far as traditions go. How do you celebrate birthdays? If you have no traditions, then you should make them up

together. Maintaining traditions respects and honors the lives you lived before you and your spouse got married.

That's it.

Tip # 175

Forget about keeping up with your ex

Sometimes you have the money and sometimes you won't. Sometimes you will get the call from your ex and they will tell you what they are doing with the children over the Winter Break. What that statement instantly does is make your spouse feel like needing to keep up with the Joneses. From gifts, trips, vacations and everything in between, trying to keep up with your ex is always a losing battle.

Plus, it causes friction in your marriage.

There's no use in playing games so make a point not to play them. Children with divorced parents frequently see one parent as wealthier or more relaxed and the other as poorer or stricter. That's a divide. Anywhere that a child can split parents the situation is unhealthy.

This is where having values very grounded comes to your rescue. If your top value is accountability, then you'll remain accountable to your words and actions.

Instead of responding negatively about your ex, you can say that you're so happy that he / she is spending time with them in this fashion. No more and no less. Feel genuinely happy for them.

Tip # 176

Master transitions

We know that children go through a lot of transitions throughout their childhood. For children in blended families, this could mean a transition every week as they're moving from one house to another. Our advice is to create a ritual and routine around these transitions. Whether you're saying hello or goodbye to the children, you need a transition plan.

Start by asking these 5 questions:

1. How are we going to transition?
2. Will we always do it together?
3. Will just one of us do it?
4. Will I go when you transition your children?
5. Will you come when I do it to mine?

Every blended family has their transition plan based on their situation.

After you establish this plan, start to create rituals and routines around getting the children.

We really encourage having family meetings at every transition. Use this as your time to check-in with your children, even if you talk to them frequently on the phone during off-weeks. Many parents don't get the highest quality conversations from phone conversations because children aren't big phone talkers.

A family meeting strengthens your family and your marriage. Meet all the time. See that both parents are interested and invested in how everyone is doing. Everyone has a voice.

Children will soon understand that every time they go from this mom's or dad's house to the other's, they have parents and Blended parents to connect with. That's powerful.

Tip # 177
Make schedules

Whether you like it or not, blended families run on schedules. You better make some. Your life will live by schedules because you've added more moving parts to the equation. Oh, and you've got extended family that still wants to visit your children.

Blended families need to schedule, at a minimum, space for these 4 things.

1. Time to all be together
2. Time to be with just your children
3. Time to be with just their children
4. Time to be alone as a couple

Let's pause here.

Question #4 is when couples stop and look at us in confusion. They ask, **"Where is there time this month to be alone as a couple?"**

We understand. But here's why you need to make alone time...
Off-weeks tend to become catch-up weeks from built up stress. You rarely make the best use of your time during off-weeks. You're getting back into your routine and your swing of things.
It's not good for marriages.
Parents ask us if it's ok to have a babysitter on the nights that they have their children. Most people's knee-jerk reaction to that question is NO WAY!
You only see your children 50% of the time, how can you possibly justify taking a night away from being with your children?
We don't know that there's a right or wrong way around that because every situation is slightly different. Regardless, it's worth asking this question and discussing it openly.
Many of our clients take a few hours to go do something as a couple — attend an event, movie, dinner — even on the nights they have their children. It's ok.
Alone time also carries some mental health benefits, too.
Half the month you've got your children to manage.
A lot of children = a lot of stress.
Taking 2 or 3 hours **"off"** to go out to dinner or go for a walk reinforces your marriage and status as a couple.

Tip # 178

Know that you will see your spouse differently
Sometimes your new spouse is stricter than you ever imagined. Sometimes they feel like they need to compensate for a dad's lack of structure and relaxed style of discipline.
And dad responds by saying the same thing.
Hence begins the dynamic stress of the blended family marriage.
You will absolutely see your spouse in a different light once you officially blend your families.
As a general trend, dads have a harder time setting rules. This could be because rule setting wasn't their role in the previous marriage.
Now he's mom and dad. He's everything.
In terms of guilt, dads seem to carry more guilt from the stress of the

divorce. Now he has a new marriage and all these new children. Guilt drives a lack of follow through on rules.

On the flipside, moms often carry multiple roles. It's not as striking for them to fill the everything role.

Solve this discrepancy by talking about your parenting style to your spouse. Key questions to ask:

1) What was your established parenting style in the previous marriage?
2) What's working for you?
3) What's not working for you?
4) What's working for your children?
5) When we get married, do you want to see that change?
6) Do you want to be more nurturing/disciplinarian?
7) Where do you want to grow as a parent?

Tip # 179
Build Household Rules

Think of your shared list of values as the foundation on which to build your household rules.

We recommend you cover these household rules **before** you get married:

1) Whose house will we move into?
2) What are the rules going to be around chores, TV time, homework, sports, and curfew?
3) What are the consequences of not following the rules?
4) Does everyone have their own room?
5) Will you share rooms?

(In our experience of working with blended families, moving into a brand-new home is best. Children become territorial when one family moves into another family's house).

The reason behind building household rules relates back to the following concept. When you're with your family of origin, your life unfolds, and you roll with it. In a blended family, you just don't get that luxury.

When you're with a blended family, your marriage begins with a 3, 8,

9, 13, and 15-year-old in your life. BOOM! Toddlers, pre-teens, and adolescents all under the same roof.

You don't have any history with their childhood. You don't have time to slowly build relationships with the children.

It takes an incredible amount of planning to make the roll-out of blended family rules successful but determine those rules early and stick to them.

Tip # 180

Create a shared list of values with your blended family

One of the reasons why therapists see patients is from them not having shared values.

Couples of blended families come into our office. They say: we're struggling. We say: let's create a list of shared values.

Sometimes it's easy. Sometimes it's not. Often people share a common list of values already, but the order of importance differs. For those with a monster list of values, typically only the top few on the list get our daily attention.

Once you create a list of shared values, try to identify the top 3. Then make it tangible. Match those values to everyday actions — as an individual, as a couple, and as a blended family.

Believe it or not, this exercise challenges people. But do it and you're working your way to blended family bliss.

Recipe for a Perfectly
Blended Family

1. Combine 2 families and traditions.
2. Enfold in Love.
3. Stir in a heaping measure of crazy schedules.
4. Add feelings and strain.
5. Chill with patience and respect.
6. Mix in honest communication (do not substitute ESP).
7. Pour on fun and new experiences.
8. Whip together, until "his" and "hers" become "ours".
Yield: One new, strong blended family!

The Jefferson Family

Tip # 181

Prepare for relationship changes

If you had a positive relationship with the child of your partner, it WILL get strained once you become a Blended parent.

Before the marriage you might have a positive relationship with your partner's children. People sometimes feel a little sigh of relief. **"Yes! I really hit it off with my partner's children!"**

It's unusual that the sentiment stays positive. It's much more usual to see strains in the relationship with children, simply because the roles change.

Parents of blended families question their level of discipline. Maybe they don't agree with their wonderful new partner's parenting style.

…He always lets them get away with this…

…She always lets her stay on the iPad…

All of a sudden, you're no longer there for fun and to impress one another. You walk into a new role. Do you discipline, or do you remain a casual bystander? The strain from these relationship changes challenges blended families.

Tip # 182

In every circumstance of divorce, there needs to be forgiveness for both parties. The bitterness of divorce has eaten at many families for too long. There is such a need for spoken forgiveness over each person touched by divorce. Speak forgiveness to your ex-spouse, no matter the circumstance. This forgiveness is not for their benefit, although it may very well have a spiritual impact long term. This forgiveness is for you and for your family. Bitterness is an ugly bedfellow. It eats away at our days and steals the joy of our nights. Loss also demands that forgiveness enter in. A huge part of mourning is feeling as though someone was stolen from you, dealing with the questions of why, and coming before God to let Him tend our broken hearts. Grace reigns when forgiveness lives.

Speak the knowledge and the truth of forgiveness over your children. They need to know that forgiveness reigns not only in eternity but today as well. Help your children speak what troubles their hearts from the divorce or loss. You would be so surprised at their takeaways. Let them know that any question is welcome. Let them ask hard stuff about life and about God. Pray over them in their beds and at the table. God will work His grace in them, even when all you see is anger, fear, or adolescent angst.

Tip # 183
Emotions
Children in blended families are more likely to be troubled simply because they experience conflict within the home plus conflict from interhousehold issues.

In addition, the youngsters - and often the adults - in blended families are grieving, but most often are not mature enough to explain why they are unhappy. Instead, their discontent shows up in negative actions and attitudes. To be honest, it's hard enough for adults to verbalize their true feelings. Most of them have lost - through death or divorce - a biological parent. They often must move to a new dwelling away from their friends, school, neighborhood, mosque or church. They bring this grief and loss into a new situation where the stress of adjusting to new rules and expectations can sometimes be overwhelming...

You must allow their losses to be mourned:

By the time of a second marriage, it is often a child's third family unit, the first being the biological parents' marriage, the second being a separate or single-family unit and the third being the new relationship which involves a Blended parent. Children need parental permission and understanding to grieve these losses, before embracing the new family system. Failure to accept mourning as a natural feeling may result in angry outbursts and potential alienation.

When the inability of family members to cope with the enormous change thrust upon them supersedes the joy developing in the blended home, family members begin to feel trapped. This hopeless state opens the door for emotions to escalate or plummet out of control for everyone. Rage, jealousy, blame, substance abuse, despair, are the usual ingredients in a pretty volatile mix.

Many feel 'unwanted', uncherished, even unloved. **Being unwanted is the worst disease that any human being can ever experience.**

Nowadays we have found medicine for leprosy, and lepers can be cured. There's treatment for TB, and consumption can be cured. But for being unwanted, unless there are willing hands to serve and there's a loving heart to love, we don't think this terrible disease can be cured.

Tip # 184

In most cases, people in a blended family have experienced divorce. That means your children have already witnessed a failed marriage. As their role model, you need to show them a successful marriage—not another failed one. Think of it this way: raising children is a temporary assignment in life. Your children will leave home one day. They will grow up and **"graduate"** from your care, but your marriage should last for a lifetime.

Spouses who neglect their marriage for their children are in for a lot of heartache. When the children grow up and leave home, those spouses only have a shell of a marriage remaining. Their children will not have had a successful marriage to emulate when they get married. Not only will your marriage suffer but marriages in the next generation will suffer.

Tip # 185

Look for people who can support you.
You might look for a therapist or a coach. Or you might find a support group of people who are going through the same challenges you are. Getting input from an objective third party may be exactly what you need, since you may be too close to the situation to make the best decision(s).

Tip # 186

As children change, you must adjust
As children grow, they go through major life changes. This means your parenting needs to change as well. You may notice the children acting out to test the new family dynamic. Don't take this personally. Stay flexible and ride the tide, knowing that you will need to make mid-course corrections along the way.

Tip # 187

Give relationships time to develop slowly and naturally.
Don't be in a hurry. You can't force one person to like or love another person. But you can urge Blended family members to get to know each other better. Give the Blended members time to get to know each other and don't try to mix it up too quickly. The more experiences they share – and the more time they live together – the more you help them form lasting bonds.

Tip # 188

Give family members permission to express their feelings.

Blended families are often weighed down with guilt and insecurity as well as confusing emotions. By giving family members the freedom to feel, grieve, love and act, you help them release built-up tension. Suggest to family members that they take care of themselves by exercising and spending time with friends.

Tip # 189

Focus on respecting, communicating, and empathizing for all involved.
This means you need to watch more carefully for sensitivities and tones of conversations, especially with the children. While you cannot make blended families love each other, you can make serious strides toward respect and constructive behavior.
Start with leading by example.

Tip # 190

Start with a positive attitude and realistic expectations.
Accept the fact that this won't be easy. You'll have frustrations and challenges. Surveys of remarried couples with children show that children are the number one reason for conflict between remarried couples. If you take the right steps and if you are willing to work, the result can be a loving, caring, supportive family of blended and biological children. Blending your families can be your second chance at success.

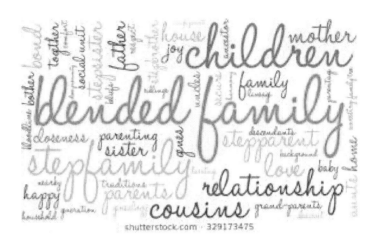

shutterstock.com · 329173475

Tip # 191

Allowing Blended-parents to discipline their step-children is one of the most common mistakes we see in newly blended families. In some cases, parents want the blended family to function just as the original family did. In others, biological parents feel overwhelmed by the demands of parenting and want a partner to share the responsibility. Some others worry that if a parent does not discipline a child, the child will not respect them. But here's the bottom line: Disciplinary decisions are the sole responsibility of the child's biological parents. Blended parents have no disciplinary role. Here's why: By the time we start disciplining our biological children, we've had years to develop a relationship with them. Over the years, that closeness helps balance the inevitable distancing that follows discipline. In other words, a healthy relationship helps cushion the blow of discipline. When a Blended-parent disciplines a Blended-child without that relationship cushion, they are bound to alienate that child forever. The parent-child relationship required for healthy and effective discipline takes years to develop and cannot be rushed.

Tip # 192

"Pushing" relationships
Many of the blended families who come to us for help make the same

mistake: Trying to force the new family members to like each other. It's an instinct, of course. A divorced mother wants her children to like her new husband. A divorced dad wants his children to like their new Blended-siblings. A new Blended-father wants his wife's children to like him. However, parents must remember they cannot force their children to like anyone — including a Blended-parent, Blended-sibling, or an ex-spouse. After all, this change in family circumstance was not the child's choice. Instead of pushing, maintain as many of the old family routines as possible while everyone learns to adjust. Emphasize respect and allow relationships to grow at their own speed. Blending new families can be a long process, filled with trial and error. The more parents can maintain stability for their children— preserving a functional and respectful relationship with the other parent, avoiding disciplinary confusion, and not **"forcing"** them into new relationships too quickly — the better everyone will adjust in both the near-term and the long-run.

Tip # 193

Time Management

In addition to spending time with the entire family, make the effort to reserve time for you and your spouse, parent-child time, and Blended parent - Blended child time. Factoring these relationship-oriented time slots into your schedule is crucial to creating a well-balanced household. The time doesn't have to involve you and your Blended child just sitting at the kitchen table staring at each other either—volunteering to take the Blended child to soccer practice and supporting him or her during the event is a great way to get in some time with your Blended child without making it too awkward.

Tip # 194

Realistic Expectations

When creating a new blended family, don't expect too much too soon. Aim for respect from your Blended children first, and don't be offended if they don't fall in love with you immediately—forming a strong, loving relationship with a Blended child often takes time and effort. Establishing mutual respect is the first step toward fostering a deeper relationship with your Blended child—just make sure your expectations are grounded in reality. Also, doing "normal" things like eating dinner together as a family can foster more of a lasting relationship and make your Blended children feel more comfortable versus always taking them to movies or theme parks. While doing fun activities with your Blended child is great, make sure you're involved in more routine events as well.

Tip # 195
Parenting Plan

Develop a parenting plan with your spouse by going over some key issues that may arise as you co-parent. For example, decide on a general formula as to how and when to punish your child for misbehaving, how to handle your child dating someone, etc. By deciding these issues before they occur, you can assure that both you and your spouse are on the same page and can present a united front to the child. This is especially when the new spouse isn't as familiar with the intricacies of raising a child.

Tip # 196

Equal Treatment

It is crucial to treat Blended children and any other children you and your spouse have equally: be especially careful not to favor your own children or your spouse's children. The parenting plan really comes into play here, where two sets of children are becoming one blended family with new rules and consequences. Moreover, recognize differences in bonding with different age groups: although you may be harsher with older children, make sure the difference in treatment is truly age-based and not just different because they are or aren't your Blended children.

Tip # 197

Take a step back

Assume a secondary role at first when you marry someone with children instead of trying to immediately become the authoritative figure. For the first year or two, consider trying to remain the secondary parent as you and your children adjust to your new blended family. Additionally, be prepared for the inevitable **"you're not my parent"** comment as well—one way to handle this situation is to explain that, while you are not their parent, you are the **"adult in charge"** and should be respected. After enough time has passed, you can assume a more primary role, but take a step back at first to ensure a smoother transition.

Tip # 198

The most important relationship to nurture in any Blended family is between the adult partners. In fact, putting more energy and effort into coupledom may improve your relationships with all the children, who will begin to see you as a strong, united front instead of two bewildered (or even squabbling) individuals.
To accomplish this goal, you need to set aside time alone with your partner to discuss family issues. At each meeting, pick the two most important problems you've been having and brainstorm solutions. At the end of each meeting, do something special: Give each other backrubs, or watch a movie to reward yourselves. And schedule regular date nights and weekends away when child-related topics are off limits. All this planning, scheduling, and communicating is tough but worth it. Learning from past relationship mistakes makes couples in Blended families better able to weather family storms. We know that you need to work hard to make a happy marriage and family.

Tip # 199

The key to developing a well-blended family is to take the time to nurture the new relationships while also communicating frequently with your spouse. You are not always going to get your way because that is unrealistic. But if you and your spouse can come to agreement on major issues, you can stop divorce from impacting yet another

family.
Many Blended families decide they need help with molding the new family into a happy unit. A Blended family can take advantage of counseling sessions to keep communication lines open. There are also classes that can be taken which discuss the special issues related to Blended families. You don't have to despair that your marriage is doomed because the children won't cooperate, or your new spouse is unsupportive. You can develop a parenting plan together, build a loving relationship over time with the Blended child, and prevent those problems which can lead to divorce.

Tip # 200

Prioritize your marriage
Just because this isn't your first rodeo with marriage (or your spouse's) and there are Blended children in the mix, does not mean your marriage gets pushed towards the bottom of the totem pole. In our home, we put God first, spouse second, and children third. These are very traditional values, and just because you don't have a traditional family doesn't mean you don't get to apply these values to your household. Don't let divorce guilt rule the roost. Put your marriage first. If your daily decisions are centered around the children's wants or demands, chaos will ensue.

Bonus: Children thrive on the security of knowing there is a pecking order and that parents are in charge.

The Wali Marriage Services:
If all you do is bury your head in your phone—texting and surfing

Facebook when you're together—it can be tough to communicate with your partner effectively, if at all. If communication breakdowns are killing your intimacy, marriage counseling can help get things moving in the right direction. Communication is the foundation of a healthy relationship. Call us at 770-256-8856 if we can help!!

Because there is no doubt that your feet are killing you right now...
Call 770-256-8856 if we can be of service.

Al Mu'mim -

The Believer Counseling Services

**Brother Marcus,
Head Counselor**

**A Fee Based Service that covers personal
counseling in a wide variety of Fields:**
"Making the Next Move in My Life"
"Issues with my Mother / Father / Sister /
Brother"
"Becoming a better Me"
"Questions to help me understand myself better"
"Dealing with something in my Past"

These and other issues in your life can be RESOLVED. Talk to someone
who cares what you are going through. Call us at 770-256-8856 and
lets talk about what happened so we can deal with it!
100% Confidential. Your business is your business!

So many of you have asked for this and I feel compelled to provide
this service. It is called the Believer Counseling Service. We provide a

100% confidential environment to help you deal with your personal issues. Your business is your business! Talk to someone who cares what you are going through. Call us at 770-256-8856 and let's talk about what happened so we can deal with it!

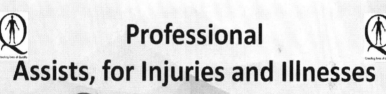

Bring us in for a Marriage Improvement Seminar or a Singles Success Workshop! We provide the latest, cutting edge information that will help you to be more successful in what you are doing. Give us a call at 770-256-8856 and let's set it up!

Marriage Empowerment Seminars

Marital Assessments How Am I doing? What can I do better?

We are able to come to your city and work with the Couples you provide us! Call 770-256-8856 and lets set it up!

Singles Success Seminars

* We get Singles to talk with each other.
* You will learn what the benefits are to having them in your life.

We are able to come to your city and work with the people you provide us! Call 770-256-8856 and lets set it up!

Made in the USA
Columbia, SC
23 May 2024

35620764R00074